Taming and Training Cockatiels:
A New Approach

Nikki Moustaki

D0595677

T.F.H. Publications, Inc.
One TFH Plaza
Third and Union Avenues
Neptune City, NJ 07753

This book has been published with the intent to provide accurate and authoritative information in regard to the subject matter within. While every precaution has been taken in preparation of this book, the publisher and author assume no responsibility for errors or omissions. Neither is any liability assumed for damages resulting from the use of the information herein.

ISBN 0-7938-0585-6

Printed and bound in the United States of America

www.tfh.com

Printed and Distributed by T.F.H. Publications, Inc.
Neptune City, NJ

Contents

The cockatiel's many positive qualities have long made it a popular companion bird.

CHAPTER 1

An Introduction to Taming and Training Cockatiels

The cockatiel, as a companion, seems to have it all. Its size and noise level makes it a perfect pet for those people living in an apartment, and it lives well in a colony setting for those who have more room to spare. The cockatiel is a highly trainable animal and adjusts well to living with humans. It can be exceptionally friendly, wanting nothing more than to sit on its owner's shoulder all day and watch the world go by.

Each cockatiel has different personality quirks, just as each human has them. Some cockatiels will take readily to strangers, while others will fear someone new. Some will defend their cages and stay inside even when the cage door is open, while others will bang the door repeatedly to get out. Wild cockatiels are active birds, but the captive cockatiel is an extremely toned-down version of its wild cousin. Some companion cockatiels are content to sit on their perches all day, munching on seed. This is why it's important for the cockatiel owner to provide a great deal of stimulation and activity for this pet. Training is just one of the many activities that your cockatiel will enjoy.

Taking care of all of your cockatiel's needs is the only way to ensure that it is trained to its optimal potential. Making sure that it has the proper housing, health care, diet, grooming, and so on, allows the bird to be relaxed and happy in its environment.

COMPANIONSHIP

When a cockatiel loves you there is no question of its affection. The human/cockatiel bond can be a strong one. Cockatiels make especially good companions when they are acquired as hand-fed youngsters. The sweeter you want your cockatiel to be, the more you

With lots of attention and handling, a cockatiel will form a strong and loyal bond to its owner.

will have to play with it. Cockatiels that get a lot of hands-on attention become intensely bonded to their human companions. A cockatiel that is left alone for too long may begin to lose its pet quality and can be come indifferent or nippy. This is why the cockatiel is a good pet only when its human companion is going to maintain a consistent amount of time spent with the bird.

The cockatiel shows its affection to its human companion by doing a number of strange-seeming behaviors. It will preen its human's hair, and it will try to kiss its human on the mouth (this is not recommended, as the human mouth contains bacteria that isn't good for a cockatiel). A male cockatiel will often regurgitate to its human as a sign of ultimate affection—the notion of vomiting as affection is ghastly, but it's actually a very charming gesture! An affectionate cockatiel will hide in its human's clothes or underneath long hair, and it may even fall asleep there—that's a sign that your cockatiel is very comfortable with you.

INTELLIGENCE

The cockatiel is an intelligent individual, able to figure out how to escape from its cage or a box, and able to solve puzzles involving a hidden treat. However, the cockatiel is not the easiest bird to teach complicated tricks to. Take heart, however, that what the cockatiel lacks in the ability to learn flashy tricks, it makes up for in loyalty and affection.

NOISE LEVEL

A cockatiel is not a noisy parrot, but noise is a subjective thing. Cockatiels will rarely annoy neighbors the way a conure or a macaw might, though a cockatiel in full squawk can cause quite a racket.

The more cockatiels you have the noisier they will be. One cockatiel will whistle and call you; two will whistle more and call each other; more than two and there will be entire conversations going on—it may be difficult to hear yourself think!

MESS

As with most parrots, cockatiels are messy. There will invariably be seeds all over your floor. Bathing is a messy affair as well, and it leads to sprinkled water all over the cage and surrounding area. And then there's always the *poop factor*, meaning that poop will manage to find its way into very unlikely places. If you are infuriated by mess, or are a die-hard neatnik, a cockatiel may not be the pet for you. There are cage accessories and acrylic cages that help to prevent mess, but there's nothing that will eliminate it.

Cockatiels are also known for producing *cockatiel dust*, a byproduct of the powder down feathers that grow close to a cockatiel's skin. This dust helps keep the feathers clean and in shape. The dust can irritate owners with allergies, but there are ways to cut down on the dust to help clear the air. Regular bathing of your cockatiel and investing in a good air purifier should help to keep the dust at a minimum.

Be certain that you have enough time to dedicate to a new pet, because a cockatiel that is ignored will be unhappy and will not thrive.

Although the initial cost of a cockatiel is comparatively low, you'll need to factor in future expenses such as food, veterinary visits, and housing and accessories.

EXPENSES

Even though you may purchase a cockatiel for a reasonable price, it's the cage and the accessories that get you in the pocketbook. Once you make the initial purchases, however, upkeep of a cockatiel (or a pair) is fairly inexpensive. Keep in mind that cockatiels can be destructive, and if you don't take precautions, a single cockatiel can damage antiques or other expensive items. This is why it's important to "cockatiel-proof" your home before you begin living with your new pet.

Here's an idea of the potential cost of keeping one cockatiel as a pet.

* Cockatiel: $25.00 to $200.00 or more
* Housing: $85.00 and up
* Accessories: $100.00 and up
* Feed: $20.00 plus (a month)
* Veterinary visit (well-bird checkup): $27.00 and up
* Emergency veterinary visit: $50.00 and up
* New drapes: $40.00 and up
* Restoration of priceless artwork: variable

TIME CONCERNS

A cockatiel is not a fish. This seems an obvious statement, though many bird owners treat their birds as if all that was needed for their proper care was a daily feeding and water change. A cockatiel, unlike a fish, needs a good deal of attention to maintain a certain level of pet quality and mental health. A cockatiel that is ignored may become unhappy and neurotic and begin to mutilate itself by picking out or chewing its feathers or other parts of its body. Even cockatiels that live in pairs need your attention as well. An observant owner who takes the time to notice the behavioral patterns of his or her birds is an owner that can prevent illness and save lives.

An Introduction to Taming and Training Cockatiels

It also takes a good bit of time to provide the daily and weekly care that a cockatiel needs to remain healthy. Cage and accessory cleaning might add up to four hours or more a week. Cleaning the mess that a cockatiel makes takes time as well. There might be times when you will have to cancel a social outing or take half a day off of work to take your cockatiel to the veterinarian in the case of an illness or accident. A person with a heavy work schedule or someone that travels frequently may not have the time required to properly take care of this pet.

RESPONSIBILITIES

As with any pet, a certain set of responsibilities come with living with a cockatiel. These responsibilities should be welcomed—a cockatiel provides its owner with more than 20 years of companionship, and an owner should be willing to provide his or her pet with what it needs to live out its life in comfort, health, and happiness.

Here's a list of the many responsibilities that come with cockatiel ownership:

* Daily cleaning of the cage.
* Weekly, a more thorough cleaning of the cage and surrounding area.
* Offering fresh water at least twice a day.
* Offering and refreshing fruits, vegetables, and safe table foods daily.
* Offering safe playtime out of the cage daily.
* Watching closely for signs of illness and taking your cockatiel to the veterinarian if you suspect something is wrong with it or in the event of an accident.
* Cockatiel-proofing your home so that it's a safe place for your cockatiel to play.
* Watching other pets closely when your cockatiel is out of its cage.
* Checking the cage and toys daily for dangerous wear-and-tear.
* Making sure your cockatiel is neither too warm nor too cold, and is housed in a spot that is free of drafts.

YOUR COCKATIEL'S NEEDS

A cockatiel's needs are many but they are easy to provide, though sometimes time consuming. A cockatiel needs proper housing and nutrition, time out of the cage and/or room to fly, a safe place to play and things to play with, a companion other than its owner if the

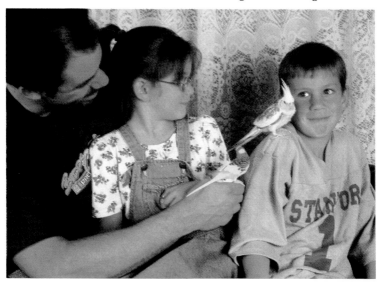

Before deciding on a bird, consider the other animals and family members in your house—be certain a new pet will be welcomed.

cockatiel is not a hands-on pet, veterinarian visits (even when well), and an observant, devoted owner—you.

Cockatiels are quirky birds with very distinct likes and dislikes. If you were to ask your cockatiel its preferences, it would probably answer a little like this:

I like room to fly; a lot of time out of my cage; wooden toys; sunshine—but not too much; millet spray; to be scratched on the head (when I'm in the mood for it); material for chewing; fruits and vegetables; music (soft jazz or classical music is nice); whistling and having my owner whistle back; scattering my seed all over the floor; shiny objects; bells; bathing in my water dish.

I dislike drafts; cold weather; extreme heat; plastic perches; the veterinarian (though I know I have to go!); loud, sudden noises; being cooped up; complete darkness at night (I tend to thrash around my cage if it's too dark and I become frightened); being ignored; people who don't know me sticking their fingers or other objects in my cage; fumes of any kind; cats.

COCKATIELS AND CHILDREN

Cockatiels do make good pets for children because the cockatiel is even tempered and tends not to be as nippy as some of the other birds in its size and price range. However, the cockatiel's beak is tough and sharp, and little fingers can be very sensitive to the occasional nip. The cockatiel may be a good pet for an older child, say, those over the age of ten, who are able to understand that the cockatiel is a little individual with likes and dislikes of its own, and that it may not always want to play when the child is ready.

Children have a tendency to have a short attention span, and they may become disinterested with the cockatiel over time. This is a sad state for the cockatiel, which will bond closely with the child and will not take well to being ignored. Also remember that a child will grow up during the cockatiel's lifetime and may move on to bigger things, like college or marriage, and she may not be able to take the cockatiel along. A child that receives a cockatiel at ten years of age might have that cockatiel until she is an adult of 30 or older!

Before a cockatiel becomes a child's pet, make sure that the child understands the nature of the responsibilities he or she will have to undertake with this creature. Make a daily checklist and post it on the refrigerator or near the cockatiel's cage and have the child check off the duties as they are performed. Depending on the child, you will have to make sure that the bird is actually being cared for. When you offer a pet to a child, it is important that you realize that you may have to eventually become the sole caretaker of the pet.

Cockatiels are only good gifts for children (or anyone, for that matter) when it is a cockatiel that the recipient desires. No child asking repeatedly for a puppy wants to receive a cockatiel—the child may become resentful of this replacement pet and take out that resentment on the bird. If you really want to give a child a pet as a gift, buy a gift certificate to your local pet shop and let your child choose his or her own pet—with limitations, of course. You could end up taking home an iguana rather than a cockatiel, but

Children and cockatiels are a good match, though an older child may be better able to help with the chores that come along with a pet bird.

at least your child will have gotten the animal he or she wanted, rather than being forced to care for an unwanted pet.

If you are going to give a cockatiel as a gift, try not to bring the animal into the home when there's a lot of hustle and bustle, such as on a birthday or major gift-giving holiday. The bird will be confused and frightened by all of the commotion and may be neglected while the festivities are going on. Again, this is a better time to give a gift certificate, or take give a photo of the gift bird and pick it up from the store when the holiday is over.

COCKATIELS AND OTHER PETS

Cockatiels have a tendency not to get along with other pets—a huge consideration in the case of people who have many other animals in the house. A fierce bird of another species may harm the cockatiel, which won't be able to defend itself well.

Cockatiels can fall prey to just about any other pet you may own. A dog or cat is deadly for the little cockatiel, which will be seen as prey or a toy by these other animals. One little scratch during "play" is enough to kill a cockatiel. Ferrets and pet rats will hunt your cockatiel, and a fish tank or bowl poses a drowning threat if your cockatiel is allowed free in your home.

If you have other pets, make sure that they either get along well, as in the case of other birds, or that they

If you foresee a time when you won't be able to give a single bird the attention it needs, consider getting more than one cockatiel, to keep each other company.

Most people will choose a young bird for a new pet, but don't overlook older birds or those with special needs, such as this 16-year-old feather-plucked male.

do not have the chance to "get together," in the case of dogs and cats. Never, ever think that it's "cute" to introduce your cockatiel to a predator—this is just asking for trouble. A fully flighted cockatiel (one without its wings clipped) may be better able to keep itself away from predators in your home, though a cockatiel that has full flight can run into other dangers.

FINAL CONSIDERATIONS

Many people think that just because they are small, cockatiels cannot get lonely or anxious. This is a fallacy; cockatiels need as much attention and care as any other bird. A lonely or mistreated cockatiel can develop illnesses and self-mutilating behaviors, which can be deadly. If you do take on a cockatiel as a pet, think ahead to what you're going to be doing in your life. Are there going to be any major life changes? Will you be able to care for this bird in the long term? A cockatiel can live 20 to 25 years or more with the proper care. What will you be doing 20 years from now? Make a solid commitment to your bird that you will care for it for the duration of its life. If you can't commit to a close relationship with a single cockatiel, it's best to buy a pair—they will keep one another company and all you'll have to do is provide the proper diet and housing, and maintain an acceptable level of cleanliness.

CHAPTER 2

The Wild Nature of Your Companion Cockatiel

Companion birds are not really domestic animals, even though many, such as the cockatiel, have been kept in captivity for hundreds of years. Your cockatiel has many things in common with its wild cousins, everything in common, in fact, except location. Your cockatiel is essentially a wild bird living a very cushy life! Your cockatiel's behavior, nutritional needs, and desire for companionship are all part of the wild nature of your bird.

The wild cockatiel originated in Australia; since its discovery by Europeans in the 1700s it has gained an enormous amount of popularity.

The Wild Nature of Your Companion Cockatiel

A LITTLE COCKATIEL HISTORY

Europeans first discovered cockatiels in the late 1700s, during an expedition of the *Endeavour* with Captain James Cook. Of course, the Aboriginal people of Australia knew this bird well, and called it the *weero* or the *quarrion*. By the mid 1800s, the cockatiel began its popularity in European zoos, and by the late 1800s, it became a fashionable aviary species for bird owners in several European countries. By the early 1900s, the cockatiel found its way to the United States, where it soon became a popular pet. Today, the cockatiel is second only in popularity to the parakeet.

A cockatiel's flocking nature is not lost when it is kept as a pet; a captive cockatiel will still want to socialize with its "flockmates"—whether humans or birds.

COCKATIELS IN THE WILD AND IN CAPTIVITY

The cockatiel enjoys a very wide natural range of the Australian mainland, and in fact, is found in just about every part of the country, from the outback to the cityscapes. The wild cockatiel is found in flocks and is highly nomadic, always on the search for water, which is scarce in the scrublands, the habitat that makes up much of their natural range. Cockatiels are capable of flying hundreds of miles in search of a source of water. They breed in the rainy season when water and food are most readily available, and they nest in hollowed-out trees or tree limbs. The wild cockatiel is a bit smaller than domestically bred cockatiels, and is found in only the wild gray, or nominate, color. This color helps the wild cockatiel to blend well into its habitat. Hawks and other raptors often prey upon them, so camouflage is extremely important.

Your cockatiel is most likely a captive-bred bird, meaning that it was not captured and imported from the wild, but was bred in captivity. The cockatiel breeds very well in captivity, so there is no reason to import them from the wild, even if that was still legal in the

United States, which it is not—the ban on bird importation requires that all birds being sold today are either captive bred or were brought into this country prior to 1991.

It is likely that your cockatiel has a metal band on its leg. This closed band has information about your bird etched into it, including the initials of the breeder, the state where the bird was bred, the year the bird was hatched, and a number that is unique to your individual bird. This last number helps the breeder keep records of the babies. Some pet owners have this band removed, especially if it is irritating the bird or there is a chance that the band will become caught on something in the cage or aviary, causing injury to the bird. Do not ever try to remove this band yourself or you might break your cockatiel's leg. Your avian veterinarian has a special tool to remove the band. However, realize that if you remove the band, you will have no way of identifying your bird should it fly away.

THE LITTLE COCKATOO

The cockatiel's Latin name is *Nymphicus hollandicus*, which translates very roughly to "nymph-like bird from New Holland." Even though the cockatiel is the only bird in its genus, ornithological evidence shows that the cockatiel might actually belong to the same genus as the cockatoo. Certainly, the cockatiel has many of the same visual characteristics as many of the cockatoos, including similar coloring and the distinctive head crest.

Cockatiels share physical characteristics with cockatoos, including a head crest.

EATING HABITS OF THE WILD COCKATIEL

The wild cockatiel consumes a variety of plant material, including nearly 30 types of seeds, fruits, and berries. They feed primarily on the ground, and they are notorious for raiding farmers' grain fields, making them quite a pest in their native land. Because of the cockatiel's ability to forage and to go for periods of time without a good water supply, they are hardy birds in captivity, where food and water are abundant. No wonder the captive cockatiel is prone to obesity! Even though young seeds are a main staple of the wild cockatiel, dry seed should only be a small part of your captive cockatiel's diet. Too many seeds can lead to malnutrition and obesity.

The wild cockatiel feeds mainly in the hour just after dawn and again in the hour just before dusk. This is also the time when your pet cockatiel is hungriest. You can capitalize on this natural behavior by feeding the most nourishing foods at this time and limiting seeds.

The nature of captivity challenges a bird owner, who must provide a pet with stimulation, food, attention, and time outside the cage.

THE IMPORTANCE OF EXERCISE

The wild cockatiel is an active bird, whose days are filled with flying, foraging for food, playing, keeping away from predators, finding nesting sites and nesting, protecting the nest, and raising young. No doubt your companion cockatiel does not have this much to do. Your pet bird probably lives in a cage far smaller than the Australian outback! Because of this, pet cockatiels are prone to becoming too heavy, which can lead to fatty tumors and even a greatly reduced lifespan. To help your cockatiel remain fit and trim, provide it with as much exercise as possible. Flying is wonderful exercise, perfectly suited for birds, but it is not always advisable to have a cockatiel flying inside the average home. A cockatiel with its wings clipped can get exercise from flapping, playing with toys, climbing ropes and ladders, and plenty of playtime out of the cage with its owners. Walking around on the floor might seem like good exercise for your bird, but there is a risk that it can be stepped on or become a snack for the family dog. Short training sessions are also good exercise for your cockatiel, because it will have to concentrate on moving, not on picking seeds out of a dish.

WILD BEHAVIORS IN YOUR COMPANION BIRD

Your cockatiel has a lot in common with its wild cousins. Even though the cockatiel is an animal that has been kept in captivity for many years, it is not domesticated and still has all of its natural instincts intact. These are behaviors that are difficult to "train out" of your bird. They are programmed into its bird brain and no amount of training will help. But that's okay—there are things you can do to prevent or discourage annoying behaviors. Above all, remember that your bird, like you, just wants to be itself. Don't expect too much from your cockatiel. It is just being a bird, the only way it knows how.

The wild behaviors that your pet cockatiel is prone to do (and that may irritate or dumbfound you) include:

* Vocalizations: Wild cockatiels vocalize loudly around dawn and at dusk, just like a rooster. Your pet cockatiel will do the same unless you regulate the amount of light that reaches the cage at certain hours. You will not be able to stop your cockatiel from vocalizing, but you can choose the time in which it begins its daily routine. However, if your cockatiel is already used to vocalizing at a certain time of day, no amount of darkness will help—birds have very good internal clocks and will be able to tell when it's time to whistle up a storm!

* Finding a high spot: Birds like to sit in the highest spot possible because a high place makes a good, secure lookout point. Birds are prey animals, and as such, are always on the lookout for predators. You may find that your cockatiel stiffens up when your dog or cat enters the room, or thrashes when it sees a hawk overhead, even if there's a window between it and your bird. Because cockatiels forage on the ground, they are extra sensitive to sound and movement. You may find that your cockatiel likes to sit on the ceiling fan (watch out!) or on your curtain rods. There's not much you can do to remove this behavior, so buy a playpen or playstand and place it in a high spot where your bird will feel comfortable.

* Sexual behaviors: Even a single cockatiel has the natural instinct to breed, and it will try it with a toy, a coop cup, or its owner's hand. A cockatiel that is stimulated to breed may also become cranky and nippy during this time. In the wild, cockatiels breed when there's an abundance of light, food, and water. Your cockatiel has the same

programming. If your cockatiel will not give up its breeding behavior, cut down the amount of light it receives to about eight hours a day, serve water in a very small cup (to discourage bathing), discontinue bathing for a time, and remove the toy or cup your cockatiel has a crush on. When the sunlight in your part of the world begins dwindling as the clocks change in the fall, you can go back to bathing your bird.

The normal gray coloration prevails in wild cockatiels; however, mutations abound in captivity. Pictured are two lutinos and a normal pied cockatiel.

THE MANY MUTATIONS

In the wild, there is one color for cockatiels—gray. You will notice, however, that there are many colors and patterns available in the pet shop or at the breeder's home. These colors are called mutations, and they are naturally occurring deviations from the normal color. The reason we don't see these mutations in the wild is because a wild cockatiel that is any color other than gray would be an easy mark for a predator and may not live long enough to pass along its genes. In captivity, breeders single out these mutations and breed them such that new mutations develop.

Because the normal gray is the most common color, it is the least expensive in stores. The more common mutations, such as lutino (yellow) and pied, are also easily found in pet shops and come with a reasonable price tag. The rare or "fancy" mutations are more difficult to find and come at a higher price, though there is no difference in pet quality among the many mutations.

C H A P T E R   3

Choosing the Perfect Cockatiel

Choosing the perfect cockatiel might seem easy—just visit your local pet shop and choose the prettiest one. That's one way of doing it, certainly, but it's not the best, most informed way to choose a pet that will be a member of your family for many years. If you've already bought a cockatiel on impulse, don't fret—this chapter will help you in the case that you want to buy it a friend.

WHICH COCKATIEL IS RIGHT FOR YOU?

There are several important decisions that go into choosing the right cockatiel for your family. Not all cockatiels will have the characteristics you might be seeking in a companion animal. Begin by making a list of all of the factors that you wish for in a pet bird. For example, some people will want a very affectionate, hands-on pet; another person is looking for a pair of birds to watch and care for; and still another is looking for compatible aviary birds. Do you want to have to train your cockatiel to be friendly, or do you want one that will cuddle with you the first day you own it? Do you want a bird that's going to talk, or will you be content with one that simply whistles? Here are some factors you will want to consider:

HAND-RAISED OR PARENT-RAISED?

A hand-raised cockatiel, that is, one that has been taken out of the nest when it was young and hand-fed by a human, makes a far better hands-on pet than a parent-raised cockatiel does. A hand-raised cockatiel will want to play with its human companion; a cockatiel that was raised by its parents will not see a human owner as a playmate, and it may shy from contact until trained. Some people handle baby cockatiels in the nest and socialize them to humans in that way, rather than

Choosing the Perfect Cockatiel

Consider visiting a breeder to learn more about cockatiel ownership. Pictured is a mother and her two gangly young, which are in the process of feathering out.

hand-feeding them—these baby cockatiels get the best of both worlds.

Most responsible pet shops and breeders will not sell you a baby cockatiel that is still eating baby bird formula. It is not a good idea for you to try to feed your baby cockatiel by hand—if you are inexperienced with hand-feeding you can burn, asphyxiate, or cause infection and death in your baby bird. Better to leave the hand-feeding to someone who knows how to do it. Your cockatiel will not be any less bonded to you when fed by someone else. You're the one who will care for it on a daily basis, and it will come to see you as a friend if you handle it regularly with gentleness and affection. Hand-feeding socializes a baby cockatiel to enjoy contact with humans. Often, the hand-feeder will take the time to play with and hold the babies, making them very tame and sweet.

You can tell that a group of cockatiels have been hand-fed by handling them. If they don't bite, are tame and calm, and rest easily in your hands, it is likely that someone socialized them to enjoy human contact. A cockatiel that flies away from you in panic might not make the best pet, though most cockatiels are easily trained to enjoy a human companion.

Age

If you want a very affection-ate pet, it is best to buy a cock-atiel just after it has been weaned off of baby formula and is eating on its own at about eight to ten weeks. An older cockatiel can make a wonderful pet as well if it has been handled regularly and is tame and sweet. Unfortun-ately, most pet shops do not take the time to handle their cockatiel stock, so the birds often "revert" as they grow older and lose the ability to be handled easily. This is easily remedied, however, with training.

Spend some time examining your chosen bird for signs of good health: clear eyes, smooth feathering, clear nasal openings, and smooth beak.

Color

There are many different colors to choose from in the cockatiel, called *mutations*, which are naturally occurring in the cockatiel, though the primary color in the wild is gray. A wild cockatiel that is any color other than gray would have a difficult time camouflaging itself and may become an easy target for a predator—this is why you won't find yel-low or albino cockatiels in the wild—birds of these colors may not live long enough to reproduce. In captivity, however, cockatiel breeders capitalize on these mutations and raise baby cockatiels in many different patterns and hues. No one color is superior to anoth-er, though it is thought that a bird of the wild gray color is a bit hardier than some of the mutations—this may be because many of the mutations are often inbred.

Some of the mutations, such as pied or lutino (yellow), are so com-mon that their price is comparable to the wild gray color, while some other, newer mutations are far more pricey. You might find a rather "dull" looking cockatiel priced much higher than a "prettier" bird—this is because cockatiel fanciers prize the different mutations and because a "dull" looking cockatiel can lend its genes to a mate to produce stunning babies of various colors. If you intend to breed your cockatiel, you may want to invest in the rarer mutations, which you will be able to find at bird shows or through serious cockatiel breeders.

Recycled Cockatiels

Many animal shelters and bird rescue organizations regularly have cockatiels up for adoption. You may want to put yourself on a list at your local shelter in the case that they get a cockatiel in for adoption. Remember that this bird might come with some quirks and will need extra patience and love in order for it to thrive in its new home. Change is difficult on a bird, so be aware that a recycled cockatiel might be anxious until it gets adjusted to its new owner and home.

Male or Female?

Both male and female cockatiels make wonderful pets, so there's no real reason to be concerned with choosing a baby bird before you know its sex—cockatiels don't come into their mature coloring until after their first molt, which can occur at six months to one year of age—until then, you may not be able to tell the sex of your bird. Males are more prone to talk than females, though both sexes make superior whistlers.

In the normal gray color, it is easy to tell the difference between the sexes. Both the male and female are a deep gray with a yellow

A very young cockatiel will require around-the-clock care and feeding. It's best to wait to get your pet when it is eating on its own, at about eight to ten weeks.

A reputable bird or pet store may be a good source for a healthy cockatiel. Examine the birds and their surroundings carefully before making a hasty purchase.

face and bright orange face-patch. However, the female has far less yellow on her face, and her orange face-patch is covered over with a wash of gray, making her colors more muted. She also has barring on the underside of her tail feathers, as do the females in many of the mutations—this barring is a good indication that your bird is a hen.

Number of Birds

A single cockatiel can make a better hands-on pet than cockatiels kept in a pair, though most well-trained cockatiels do not lose their pet quality when kept with other birds; however, cockatiels in pairs are less likely to mimic human speech than the single cockatiel. In the case of a single cockatiel, you act as its "mate," providing the love and affection it needs to be happy. Keeping one cockatiel alone in a cage with no human or bird contact is cruel. If it happens that your pet is not getting the attention you once provided due to a lifestyle change, consider getting it a friend.

WHERE TO ACQUIRE YOUR COCKATIEL

For many people, the cockatiel is an impulse buy from a pet shop, a purchase made with the heart. Often, buyer's remorse sets in once the owner learns of all the details involved with caring for a bird, the bird gets aggressive and bites, or becomes ill and dies due to the purchase having been made at a non-reputable store. Buying the right cockatiel, one that's healthy and properly socialized to humans, is easy once you've found a shop or a breeder that cares for their young birds correctly.

Most pet shops carry a variety of birds along with their other animals. The store employees may not have a vast knowledge of birds and may not know much more about a particular bird than its price. The staff at a large general pet shop may not be able to recognize the signs and symptoms of illness in a bird, will know little about the history of a particular bird, and will not have spent much time playing with the birds in their care. If you buy your cockatiel from a general pet shop, the responsibility might be on you to choose the best bird of the bunch, though some larger stores do employ staff to deal exclusively with their bird stock. If you sense that the employees are knowledgeable about birds, the birds seem well cared for, the cages are clean, and all of the birds have fresh food and water, then it may be safe to make the purchase there. Pet shops that keep their birds in unclean conditions, locked away in tiny cages, are more likely to sell you an ill bird that has not been properly socialized or that has lost its pet-ability. In this case, buyer beware.

A shop that sells only birds and bird supplies might be a better place to find your cockatiel. The staff in the bird shop deals only with birds and troubleshoots bird problems with customers all day long. They are trained to know how an ill bird behaves, and they may know something about

Think carefully before deciding on a bird—with good care a cockatiel can live to be 25 years old.

the history and personality of your particular bird. Often, bird shops are willing to provide a new owner with a health guarantee, and they require a visit to the veterinarian to make the guarantee complete. It is heartbreaking to purchase a cockatiel only to have it die in the first few weeks of ownership. This is why a visit to the veterinarian soon after the purchase is so important—it will show that the place of purchase is responsible for any illness the cockatiel may have brought home with it. Always ask for a health guarantee before buying a bird, and get it in writing before you leave the store.

Perhaps the best place to buy a cockatiel is from a cockatiel breeder, one who is involved in the cockatiel fancy, someone dedicated to the species and knowledgeable about the care and training of these birds. Because cockatiels are not difficult to breed, you can often find a reputable breeder by looking in the classified ads in the newspaper or in the back of a bird magazine, or by going to a bird show or exposition. A cockatiel breeder is more likely to have the fancier mutations and might be willing to help mentor you through the trials of cockatiel ownership. This is someone who cares about the lives of their baby cockatiels and will be available to answer any questions you might have about raising your new feathered friend.

A bird rescue organization is a great place to go if you want to give a home to a cockatiel that has been given up for adoption. Sadly, most birds typically only live in a home for two years before they are shuffled along to the next place, and as a result, there are plenty of homeless birds needing a family to call their own. Do an Internet search on "rescue birds" or call your local shelter to have your name put on an adoption list.

HOW TO CHOOSE A HEALTHY COCKATIEL

A healthy cockatiel is busy and energetic, bright and attentive, is active and presents a good attitude. A healthy cockatiel sings and chirps, has bright eyes, clear nares (nostrils), a clean vent, and is free of debris on its feathers, which are tight and shiny and covering the entire bird with no patches missing. Its feet are clean and intact, and it eats with gusto. It clambers around the cage, hops from perch to perch, and seems lively in general. When it sleeps it does so on a perch, usually sitting on one leg. Choose a cockatiel that has these qualities.

A cockatiel that is not feeling well may be fluffed up and sitting on the cage floor in a corner, looking depressed. It may have a discharge from its eyes or nares and a messy vent. Its feathers might be

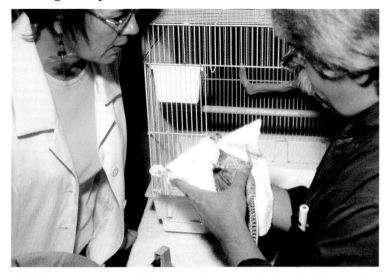

A health guarantee ensures that you can have a new bird examined by an avian veterinarian for existing conditions or diseases.

dirty from lack of grooming, and it may even have patches of feathers missing. It may look sleepy and droopy, puffing its feathers to keep in its body heat. This is not a cockatiel you want to take home, even out of pity. Let the store manager know that you believe something is wrong with this bird. It's not a good idea to buy other birds from the same store if you suspect they are selling an ill bird—many avian diseases are airborne and need no direct contact to be passed from bird to bird. Do not overlook the bird that is simply unhappy or being picked on, however—this bird may just be miserable in its present circumstance and may have feathers missing because the others are picking them out. Watch the cage dynamics closely to determine if this bird is ill or simply not suited for the hard life of a bird waiting in a pet shop for a good home.

HEALTH GUARANTEE

Always inquire about a health guarantee and get one in writing whenever you acquire a bird. If the place you are buying the bird from does not offer a guarantee, do not purchase your bird there. A health guarantee may require that you visit the veterinarian within a number of specified days—that's a good incentive to take your new bird to the doctor for a checkup.

C H A P T E R   4

Housing Your Cockatiel for Optimal Training

Many people don't like the idea of keeping a bird in a cage—birds are supposed to be free, right? Yes, that's true, but the home offers many dangers for your curious cockatiel. A cage will keep your bird safe and out of mischief when you're away. Supervised out-of-cage time is a necessary part of your cockatiel's life, but an unsupervised cockatiel might get in harm's way—and fast! Cockatiels housed in the proper kind of cage with the appropriate accessories often love their cages and think of them as "Home Sweet Home." A cage is not meant to be a prison, but a safe space for your bird to reside while you're unable to supervise it.

IMPROPER HOUSING: BUYER BEWARE

To begin a discussion of proper cages, we should first take a look at improper cages. Bamboo or wooden cages made to house finches and canaries are attractive but unacceptable for the cockatiel. Cages shaped like pagodas are too tall and narrow for the cockatiel, which likes a lot of horizontal space to clamber around in—cages with more vertical space than horizontal space are wasted on the cockatiel. Tiny, ornate, showy cages are inappropriate as well—these are best for decorative wooden birds. Elaborate scrollwork on a cage can catch toes or leg bands, causing serious injury. Cages with bars painted or covered with plastic or other materials are a terrible choice for the cockatiel, which will spend the day picking the material off of the bars, which can be toxic, or at least harmful and can cause death if ingested.

Cage bars should be spaced such that your cockatiel will not be able to poke its head through them—it might not be able to get its head out again, like a child with its head stuck in a banister. A cockatiel with its head stuck will panic, which can lead to a broken neck or strangulation.

FINDING THE RIGHT CAGE

The right kind of cage isn't hard to find if you know what you're looking for. Any pet shop should carry appropriate housing for your cockatiel, but you may have pick through the selection to find what you want. Don't allow the pet store staff to push you into buying something you feel is inappropriate for your pet. A cranky, confined cockatiel will be far less easy to train than one that's happy in its home.

Proper Size

Wild cockatiels spend most of their days winging around the scrublands, searching for water, nesting, and foraging

The initial cost of setting up a cage with accessories can be substantial, so it's best to make careful, well-researched choices.

for food. A companion cockatiel lives a far different life, but its energy level can surely compete with its wild cousins'. Because of their high energy level, cockatiels need a rather large space in which to spend their days. Unfortunately, most store-bought cages are tiny and don't allow the cockatiel to expend this energy, which can be turned upon itself in the form of self-mutilation. Buy the largest cage your budget and space demands. If the cage looks like it would generously house several cockatiels, then that might be the one to purchase.

A cockatiel forced to spend its days housed in a very confined space will be extremely unhappy. Remember, birds are creatures of boundless space, and even though your cockatiel was raised in captivity, its instincts tell it that being confined is unnatural. If your cockatiel is going to spend a good portion of the day housed in a cage, be sure that you buy the largest that your space and budget can afford. The minimum length for a cockatiel cage should be at least three feet

Cages that are painted or coated with plastic can be a problem for a cockatiel, which will dedicate a good portion of its time to picking at any loose material on the bars.

(36 inches) long, though the width and height can vary from 24 inches to as large as you want. Remember, a cockatiel has a long tail that will get raked across the bars every time it turns around unless the cage is large enough, leading to a ratty-looking tail. Your bird should be able to actually fly from perch to perch—this means that it should take wing-power to get from one side of the cage to the other. Most "cockatiel" size cages only allow a wing-assisted hop, or force the bird to clamber on the bars to move around—this size cage is too small.

Proper Shape

The perfect shape for a cockatiel cage is a large square or a large, long rectangle. Corners in a cage will make a cockatiel feel comfortable and give it a tight space to crawl into when it's feeling insecure or sleepy. The bars on the cockatiel's cage should be primarily horizontal, with a few vertical bars for structural purposes. Horizontal bars allow the cockatiel to climb around its cage and hang safely on the side.

Proper Materials

The proper material for a cockatiel cage is uncoated steel or another non-toxic metal. Many cages come in a combination of metal and plastic, which is fine for the cockatiel. Acrylic cages are a nice choice for the cockatiel because the solid walls prevent mess, though they don't allow for climbing and can be quite pricey. If you are going to make a cage, be sure to scrub the caging materials well and leave them outside in the weather for a few weeks before you use them, because wire is often coated in zinc, which is deadly for birds.

Safe Doors

Commercially made cages commonly come with three types of doors. The best types of doors for the cockatiel are the doors that open downward (like an oven door) or to the side (like your front door). Doors that slide up and down (like a guillotine) are the most common type, but can cause your bird serious injury. If your cage does have this style of door, consider buying spring clips or another type of lock so that your bird can't slide the door up.

The Cage Bottom

The proper cage for a cockatiel is one that has a grating or a grill on the bottom so that the cockatiel is prevented from rolling around in its own mess. In the wild, cockatiels are never exposed to their own fecal materials the way they are in a caged environment. You should take care that your cockatiel is exposed to as little of its own waste material as possible—a grate on the bottom of the cage will help this.

CAGE ACCESSORIES

Now that you have purchased the proper cage, you have to furnish the cage with all of the necessities and goodies that your cockatiel will need to be happy and healthy. Many of these are one-time purchases and should last the lifetime of your bird.

Perches

Most commercial cages come with a couple of smooth wooden dowels as perches, which are fine to use, but they are an inadequate selection for a cockatiel, which spends most of its life on its feet. A wide variety of perches can help to maintain your cockatiel's foot health. A cockatiel that stands on the same perch day after day may develop foot sores and lameness, among other foot disorders. These are easily

Although many cages will come with water and food cups, as well as a perch or two, it may be helpful to buy additional accessories.

Your parakeet and cockatiel may get along perfectly well during supervised playtime, but it's probably best for each bird to have its own home cage.

remedied by offering various perches made of assorted materials in many different dimensions. Your cockatiel should have perches that make it stand with its feet very spread out (almost flat) and perches that allow its toes to curl around when it's gripping them. Fortunately, there are many different types of perches on the market, and they are easily found at your local pet store. Buy perches made of different types of wood, rope, and concrete for optimum foot health. A cockatiel with painful feet is less likely to be easily trainable than one whose feet don't hurt.

The sandpaper sheaths that slip over perches are not the same as concrete perches, and, in fact, are prone to causing foot problems. The sandpaper is abrasive and can cause sores, and the paper tends to get wet and hold bacteria in it—not something you want under your cockatiel's feet.

Cups

The standard commercial cage usually comes with two square, plastic cups designed to fit neatly into doors located toward the bottom of the cage. These cups are fine, but they are by no means the best choice. Plastic cups are difficult to clean, not only because the square shape does not allow thorough cleaning of the crevices, but because the plastic eventually becomes scratched, and bacteria likes to hide out in the scratches and muck up the water. A standard cage usually has places for the cups at the lower half of the cage, which might allow poop to fall into the cups, which is not sanitary. Replace plastic cups with two sets of round, stainless steel cups—this means that you will have six cups—two for water, two for seed/pellets, and two for fresh foods, though you will only use one set at a time, allowing the other set to be thoroughly washed and dried before its next use. Stainless steel is easy to clean and is very durable. Ceramic cups are nice as well, but they are easier to break and will eventually scratch.

Some people use water bottles or self-watering tubes to dispense water. These have the disadvantage of becoming clogged or dirty, and owners tend to refresh the water less frequently. A coop cup filled with clean water at least twice a day should do nicely—no need for bottles or tubes.

Toys

Toys are a must for the high-energy cockatiel—a cockatiel without toys to fling, chew, snuggle, and argue with, will be a bored and unhappy cockatiel, indeed! The single cockatiel, especially, must have many toys to play with; a pair or colony of cockatiels will still enjoy playing with toys but it is not necessarily essential for them to have as many. Toys give your cockatiel something to do while you're away and offer much-needed exercise to a cage-bound bird.

Safety first is the motto when it comes to toys for your cockatiel. Beware of toys that are flimsy or have small spaces where a toe can catch. Your cockatiel's head should never be able to fit in a ring that comes on a toy. Toys that are made for much larger or smaller birds should never be considered. Toys labeled for cockatiels and conures are usually appropriate. Rope toys and perches should be trimmed regularly once they begin fraying.

Cockatiels adore swings, so make sure that you provide your pet with at least one. Mirror toys are good for the single bird, but if you notice your cockatiel becoming too attached to its reflection you might want to take that toy away and replace it with something else, or your cockatiel might prefer its "mirror mate" over you.

Homemade toys are great when used with supervision. Toilet paper rolls cut into rings and hung on sisal rope are very entertaining, as are strung Cheerios and popcorn.

Rotating your cockatiel's toys is a great way to keep them "new" and allow you time to clean them. Buy more toys than will fit in the cage at any one time and rotate them in and out of the cage on a weekly basis. Don't remove your cockatiel's absolute favorite toy, however, as this can cause undue stress. Don't worry that toys will interfere with training—they don't.

Other Accessories

Now that you've taken care of the essential cage accessories, here's a list of other indispensable items that your cockatiel will need to thrive:

* Bird lamp: If you live in a Northern climate that is dark for much of the year, or your cockatiel lives in a room that doesn't get much light, you should invest in a bird lamp. There are many available on the market, or you can simply buy a spotlight from a hardware store and equip it with a bird or reptile bulb from your local pet store. This high-spectrum bulb provides your cockatiel with the "natural" light it needs to maintain its health. A bird kept without the proper lighting can become malnourished. You can keep the light on for nine to ten hours a day.

A cage door that opens outward is less likely to cause injury than a guillotine-style door; it also can serve as a landing platform during free time.

* Cage cover: Your cockatiel does not need its cage covered at night, though people that like to sleep a little later in the morning might do well to invest in a dark cage cover. A cover also serves to keep out drafts and to quiet noisy birds during the day. Don't use the cover, however, for extended periods of time in daylight hours—it should only be used for a few minutes to calm noisy birds in the event that you need them to be silent, for example, when an infant is taking a nap. Be careful that the cover does not become

Perches come in a variety of styles and materials; consider using a rough or concrete perch to help keep your bird's nails trimmed.

frayed or holey, both of which can injure or kill a cockatiel. If the cover is very thick, the extreme darkness in the cage may frighten a cockatiel and cause it to thrash around its cage, a phenomenon common to cockatiels—in the case that you hear flapping or distress in the cage when you cover it at night, flip up a corner of the cover and let some light through.

   • Nightlight: If your bird becomes frightened at night, or you have a cat or rodents roaming the house, you will want to keep a nightlight on in your bird room. This will give your cockatiel a sense of security—it will be able to tell the difference between a real predator and someone making a midnight snack in the kitchen.

   • Mineral block and cuttlebone: These items provide much needed calcium to your cockatiel's diet and are fun to chew and destroy. Make sure that your bird has at least one of each, and replace them when they become soiled.

   • Flooring: Your cockatiel's cage should have a metal grating on the bottom so that it can't get to its mess, but you will need to put something in the bottom of the cage nonetheless. Regular newspaper is the easiest choice, and if you change it at least every other day, it's sanitary as well. Many people use corncob or other types of litter for the cage bottom, but these tend to hold moisture.

* Bath: Your cockatiel will want to bathe and will do so in its water dish, unless you provide it with a special bath. There's no stopping your bird from bathing in the water dish, but a larger, shallow bath offered several times a week might help.

* Playgym: Your cockatiel will appreciate a cage-top playgym, complete with ladders and toys, and even a cup for snacks.

* Seed catchers: A cage bloomer or plastic seed guard goes a long way toward keeping seed inside the cage.

* Mite protectors: There is no need for this item, and, in fact, the chemicals inside can be harmful for your bird. Instead of the mite protector, take your bird to the veterinarian for a checkup. It's unlikely that your cockatiel has mites, or that it will contract them.

SETTING UP THE CAGE

1. Make sure that all of the parts of the cage are put together correctly and securely.

2. Place full food and water cups toward the front of the cage and about midway to the top. If the doors where the cups should go are too low, don't use them—use a cup holder instead.

3. Place perches at various levels toward the middle to the top of the cage, making sure that there are no perches above food or water dishes. Cockatiels prefer to be at a high point in the cage, so don't position perches too low. If you place perches above one another, they are going to become soiled.

4. Place the cuttlebone and mineral block on the sides of the cage near a perch. Don't place these items too low where they can be soiled.

5. Place toys in various spots around the cage, making sure that they don't block the food and water dishes.

6. Pull out tray and add newspaper to the bottom of the cage—below the grate.

7. Add bird (or birds).

8. Place the spring clips or locks on the doors.

You're done! Your cockatiel is home!

CLEANING YOUR COCKATIEL'S CAGE

Daily cleaning chores include changing the paper in the bottom of the cage, soaking the dishes in a 10 percent bleach solution, and making sure there are no poop deposits on the perches.

Housing Your Cockatiel for Optimal Training

Weekly chores include disassembling the cage and cleaning it thoroughly with a bleach solution or kitchen soap and a scrub brush, scrubbing all the perches and cleaning and rotating toys. A larger cage can be hosed down outside—remove cockatiels first, of course! The smart cockatiel owner invests in a good handheld vacuum.

Many household detergents and cleansers are extremely dangerous for your cockatiel. Instead, use vinegar as a disinfectant and baking soda as a cleanser (don't mix the two, however). A 10 percent bleach solution is fine as well—bleach is nontoxic to birds. Rinse everything thoroughly before putting your cockatiel back in the cage.

Keep life interesting for your cockatiel by rotating different toys in and out of the cage.

CAGE ALTERNATIVES

Because cockatiels appreciate being together and are generally peaceful among themselves and other peaceful species of birds, they make excellent colony birds and can be kept together in large aviaries. An aviary allows cockatiels to do what they do best—fly. This is a wonderful gift that you can give your birds, and anyone with any amount of space can have an aviary. Once your cockatiel is well trained, keeping it in an aviary setting will not damage that training, as long as you reinforce it daily.

CHAPTER 5

A Happy Homecoming

Once you've chosen the perfect cockatiel for you, there's the matter of transporting it home and setting up the ideal living situation for it. The pet shop will have cardboard boxes for you to transport your cockatiel home in, but you may want to get the jump on all of the equipment you will need and buy a bird carrier, one that has grating in the front or on top so that your cockatiel has a view. If you have a short ride, you don't have to bother with food and water, but if the ride is long, ask for some refreshment for your bird. Place the bird in

A new bird will need a few hours to a few days to adjust to its new surroundings; give it some time before introducing other family members.

a spot in the car that is neither too hot nor too cold, and it's best to buckle the carrier in for safety.

PLACING THE CAGE

Where your cockatiel is going to live is an important decision that can make the difference between a very happy bird and a miserable one. Your cockatiel's cage is best placed in a location that gets a lot of traffic, like the family room, living room, or the room where everyone watches television. A place where there's too much swift-moving traffic, like a hallway, isn't a great location, however. The cage should be in an area where there's a sense of relative calm, but where it is well attended by the members of the family.

Because your cockatiel

A holiday or other special occasion may be too hectic for a new bird to come home to. Consider waiting a few days for things to calm down.

needs a good deal of attention, an out-of-the-way location isn't the best choice—it will begin to miss its "flock" (you and your family) immediately if relegated to a back room. The garage is too drafty and is prone to fumes. The bathroom and kitchen are both places that are prone to wide temperature ranges and chemicals, neither of which are healthy for a cockatiel. A child's room might be dark and quiet for most of the day while the child is at school, and too noisy at other times. Again, the family room or television room is your best bet.

Once you've decided on the room where your cockatiel is going to live, choose a corner location that is free of drafts and try to make sure that the cage is covered on at least two sides by the walls of the room, which will make your cockatiel feel safe. A cage that's standing or hanging in the middle of the room will make for an extremely insecure bird. When the family cat appears or a car backfires outside, your cockatiel will want to retreat to the back of the cage—a cage that's freestanding will have no "back," no place for the cockatiel to "hide." To make your cockatiel feel even more secure, especially if you can't place the cage next to a wall, you can surround the cage with safe, nontoxic plants. Be aware that a cockatiel will make quick work of a plant, chewing it to bits, so you should carefully supervise your bird when it's out of the cage.

Don't place the cage directly in front of a window, even though this seems like the thing to do. Your cockatiel really doesn't need a view. Cockatiels are extremely alert creatures and will become alarmed by predators lurking outside—these predators can take the form of the neighbor's cat or dog, hawks circling in the sky, rats and raccoons, and even cars going by. Imagine having to be on guard all the time! Also, the sun shining in a window may overheat your bird if it can't get out of the sunlight. It's okay for your cockatiel to be placed *near* a window, but not directly in front of it, unless the cage is so large that part of it extends over onto a wall.

Placing a commercial cage outside on a patio or porch is extremely risky. For one, your cockatiel will be very vulnerable to predators outside, and a measly cage is no match for a determined raccoon or opossum. A thief might be tempted to steal your cockatiel, cage and all. The pet cockatiel housed on a patio might not get as much attention as it would housed in a family room. Some people choose to house multiple cockatiels in large cages on an enclosed patio or porch—in this case the cockatiels have one another for company and the cage is far too large for a thief to make off with it. A cage on a patio should be double-wired, that is, two layers of wire placed one over the other such that a predator would not be able to get to the feet of the birds inside—a rat or raccoon can actually pull a small bird through the wires of a cage. Also, if you live in a place that gets very hot or very cold, house your cockatiel inside.

COCKATIEL-PROOFING YOUR HOME

If your cockatiel is going to have free time out of the cage and there is the possibility of you turning your back on it for a moment, even just to answer the phone, you'd better cockatiel-proof your home. The average home presents many dangers for a cockatiel. Here's a cockatiel-proofing checklist you can follow to keep your feathered friend safe:

• Screen all windows and doors and check regularly for holes in the screening.

A Happy Homecoming

It's best to place your bird's cage in its permanent location and set it up before your new bird comes home.

* Wrap all electric wires and tuck them away.
* Put decals on all windows and mirrors.
* Remove all items containing toxic metals.
* Remove all toxic plants.
* Keep toilet lids down and remove all other standing water.
* Remove ceiling fans or keep them off.

THE MOST SERIOUS HOUSEHOLD DANGERS TO COCKATIELS

Cockatiels are curious creatures that can find trouble in nearly anything, but the following are the most common household dangers to the cockatiel.

* Predators: The family dog poses a huge threat to the cockatiel, and the family cat is an even deadlier enemy. One slight nip from a dog, even in play, can mean death for your cockatiel. Cats don't even have to bite to kill a bird—they have a type of bacteria on their claws and in their mouths that is extremely toxic to birds—one scratch and the bird will die within 48 hours unless immediate treatment by a veterinarian is sought.

* Water: Standing water is a strong temptation for a cockatiel, which may want to take a bath or drink. Unfortunately, the bird may

fall into a pool deeper than it can remove itself from. Many cockatiels drown in toilets, large dog bowls, fish tanks and bowls, half-full drinking glasses, ponds and fountains, Jacuzzis, full sinks (with dishes soaking), and pots of boiling water—this last instance is especially awful. Keep your toilet lids down at all times and keep all exposed water covered.

* Nonstick cookware: Any cookware labeled "nonstick" emits an odorless fume that, when heated, can kill a bird within a matter of moments. It was previously thought that the fumes only occurred when the nonstick surface was overheated, but research now indicates that it is emitted at even low levels of heat. Birds have tremendously sensitive respiratory systems, far more delicate than ours. If you notice that your cockatiel is in distress and there's no apparent reason, check for gas leaks or other fume-causing agents, such as scented candles, fireplaces, and heated nonstick surfaces.

Many items other than pots and pans can have nonstick surfaces. These include heat lamps, portable heaters, irons, ironing board covers, stove top burners, drip pans for burners, broiler pans, griddles, cooking utensils, woks, waffle makers, electric skillets, deep fryers, crock pots, popcorn poppers, coffee makers, bread makers, non-stick rolling pins, lollipop molds, stockpots, roasters, pizza pans, and curling irons. Even a well-ventilated room isn't safe when there are nonstick items being used.

* Common household products: Keep all household cleaning items away from your cockatiel. These

What may look like normal, everyday kitchen items are deadly hazards for a cockatiel on the loose.

include soaps, drain cleaners, laundry detergents, floor cleanser, and bathroom cleaners, all of which might be a tempting treat for your cockatiel—with tragic consequences. Items commonly kept in a garage should be stored neatly away from your bird. These include fertilizers, pesticides, and barbeque products such as charcoal and lighter fluid. Realize that your cockatiel can easily tear through paper bags. Items regularly sprayed into the air can cause severe respiratory distress or death, including air freshener, fabric freshener, and even scented candles.

Even if your dog is friendly and harmless, it could inadvertently injure your bird or, at the very least, cause it added stress.

* Toxic houseplants: Cockatiels are chronic nibblers, always shredding something to bits the moment you turn your back. Your houseplants are a serious temptation for your cockatiel, which is naturally attracted to them. Even one nibble of a toxic plant can poison your cockatiel and cause death.

* Ceiling fans: Birds have a natural instinct to climb or fly to the highest spot that they can find. A high spot is generally safe from predators and is a good lookout point. A ceiling fan seems like the perfect spot for a fully flighted cockatiel. Now, imagine a cockatiel flying around a room and a ceiling fan on—it's like a chicken in a food processor! One good whack from the blade of a ceiling fan is all it takes to bring your cockatiel down for good. Make sure all ceiling fans are kept off or have them removed.

* Open windows and doors: The threat of a fully flighted cockatiel winging out of an open door or window is a serious one—many cockatiels that take flight outdoors are never seen again. Keep all doors and windows securely closed or screened when your cockatiel is out of its cage, or make sure that its wings are clipped properly. Even if you believe that your cockatiel is attached to you and would never

leave, or that its wings are well clipped, a loud noise such as a car backfiring might frighten your cockatiel into flight, and it may become confused and not find its way back.

* Human feet and doorjambs: Cockatiels allowed to walk on the floor are in danger of being stepped on or crushed in a doorjamb.

* Toxic foods: Most foods are perfectly fine for a cockatiel to ingest, with the exception of avocado (parts of it are toxic), chocolate, rhubarb, alcohol, and caffeine. These items can make a cockatiel very ill, or even kill it.

* Electrocution: Some cockatiels like to snack on electric wires. Keep all wires wrapped and hidden away from your bird. Lamps and other plugged in appliances do not make good playgyms.

* Heavy metals: Keep your cockatiel away from stained glass decorations, costume jewelry, lead fishing weights, or other materials containing metals that can be toxic to your cockatiel. Hardware cloth, the material many people use to build cages, is often dipped in zinc to prevent rusting—this zinc is deadly for your cockatiel—rinse and scrub all homemade cage material thoroughly before housing birds.

* Temperature fluctuations: Cockatiels are sensitive to extreme heat and extreme cold—they can die from overheating and are prone to frostbite in cold, windy conditions. If you live in an extreme climate, be sensitive to your cockatiel's temperature requirements.

* Mirrors and glass: A cockatiel that has full flight will not know the difference between empty space and a clean window or mirror— these solid objects will look to your cockatiel as if it could fly right through them, with drastic consequences. This is a great excuse to leave your windows dirty, or at least to buy pretty decals to put on them.

* Human medicines: Never, ever try to treat your bird with human medicines, which may react very differently in your bird's delicate system than they do in yours. Treat your bird only with medicines provided by your avian veterinarian and prescribed to your bird.

THE FIRST FEW DAYS AT HOME

When you first bring your cockatiel home you will want to give it a few pressure-free days to adjust to the new environment. This is not the time to begin heavy training sessions or long playtimes away from the cage. Change is difficult on a bird, which is a creature that likes routine. Think of your cockatiel's life before you decided to take it home—it was bred and hand-fed in one place, sold to another place, and now is moving to a third location—that's a lot of adjustment!

First, set up your new friend's cage and place it in its permanent location. This way you won't be adding toys and cups while your cockatiel is simply trying to relax. Once you've placed your cockatiel in its new cage and given it fresh food and water, leave it alone

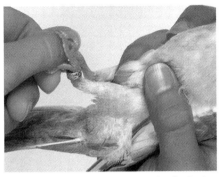

A bird's closed band can help identify a bird using specific information from the breeder and the breeder's records.

in quiet for a few hours so that it can get used to its new situation. Offer millet spray at this time. It's a good sign of adjustment when your cockatiel begins to eat and make noise.

After a day or so you can begin taking your cockatiel out of its cage for playtime. If it's a baby, gently scoop it off of the perch or side of the cage, making sure not to pull hard on its feet, which will be clutching hard to whatever it's standing on. The baby doesn't yet know to step on to your finger—you will have to teach it this command. Don't expect too much from your cockatiel at first. You're both getting used to each other.

Each cockatiel has a different personality and different favorite things. You will learn all about your new bird as the days go on. In this initial stage, move calmly around the bird and play with it very gently. This is the time to build the relationship between you, the time when your bird will learn to trust you and see you as a friend. If you force an interaction at this fragile time, you may only succeed in scaring your bird, and it will remember you as someone to be feared. If you play with your bird every day for the first few weeks, perhaps even fielding a few uncomfortable nips with composure, you'll find that your cockatiel will develop a sparkling, spirited personality and that the two of you will become fast friends. The change from baby bird to adolescent happens rapidly, and at about four to five months of age a cockatiel begins to show how fun it can be.

WING CLIPPING

To properly train a bird, its wings must be clipped during the period of training or it will simply fly away from you, making training nearly impossible. Clipping a bird's wings is the act of cutting the primary flight feathers (only the first half of the feather) so that the bird is unable to fly very high or very far. These are the only feathers on a bird that you should ever clip.

To Clip or Not to Clip

If you feel guilty about having your bird's wings clipped, you're not alone. Many people feel that wing clipping is cruel, or that it hurts the bird. In truth, clipping wings, if done properly, hurts as much as a haircut, and feathers, like hair, grow back, usually in about five months if the bird is healthy, perhaps even sooner.

Should you clip your cockatiel's wings? That depends more on your ideas about living with a companion bird than it does on your cockatiel. No bird wants its wings clipped. Birds are creatures of boundless space. Most would take the first opportunity to dash out the window for a bit of soaring time. But then what? Your cockatiel lands in a tree and sees hawks circling overhead. Cars zoom by and a neighborhood cat sharpens its claws on the trunk. Your cockatiel's flying fun has now become a tragic situation. You may never find your cockatiel again. And that's only one danger to keeping a cockatiel flighted. Fully flighted birds are more likely to burn themselves on a hot stove, drown in the toilet, or break their necks flying headlong into clean, closed windows or shiny mirrors.

Beginners to pet birds often keep their birds safer (read: alive) when they are clipped. Will your cockatiel really suffer if it is not allowed to fly? Not if you give it a lot of free time out of the cage and house it in a large space. However, flying is essential for the psychological well-being of a bird. This is an animal that is meant to fly, and when that's taken away, it can result in neurotic behaviors, such as self-mutilation. The bird will feel vulnerable and have little self-direction. Unfortunately, clipping is important for the safety of most cockatiels, and it is especially important for training. One way to avoid neurotic behavior in your clipped cockatiel is to give it as much attention as possible. You may also want to consider an aviary or habitat where your birds can fly without risk—many cockatiel owners use this option, and their birds are healthy and happy as a result.

Another option is to clip your new bird for an initial period of time, say six months to a year, until your cockatiel is very well trained. This initial unflighted period will allow your bird to become used to you and your home, to training, to your other pets, and other family members. You must come to know and trust your bird's habits before you make the decision to let its flight feathers grow out. Remember, the potential for tragedy is always there. If you can make your home absolutely safe, and you're positive that it can't escape or injure itself in any fashion, let it fly under supervision—it has wings for a reason. If you are not certain about your bird's safety, keep it clipped, but go the extra mile to provide the freedom and stimulation that it would otherwise get from flying.

How to Clip Your Cockatiel's Wings

If you've chosen to clip your cockatiel's wing feathers to prevent it from flying away, you should find a professional in your area who will clip them at first and show you how to do it yourself. Many owners are squeamish about clipping their own cockatiel's wings and choose to have someone else do it for them. If you have an avian veterinarian, he or she is the best person to clip your bird's wings. That way you have the added bonus of a veterinarian handling your bird. You can always clip the wings yourself, and you may want to learn how, especially with a cockatiel, which needs the new feathers trimmed as they grow in.

When clipping wings the first thing you must be able to do is hold your cockatiel properly. You can't grab a bird any way you want,

A cockatiel is a light-bodied bird, so a wing clip of 14 feathers is best to ensure that it doesn't fly away.

TAMING AND TRAINING COCKATIELS   **47**

Clipping should be done with a sharp scissor, one feather at a time

spread out a wing, and clip. This can be very dangerous and lead to injury. A cockatiel has fragile bones that can break if you're too rough or don't hold it properly. A bird has a different way of breathing than we do, and it's possible to prevent it from breathing by holding it around the chest area, even lightly. You should grasp the bird around the neck and the back, leaving the chest free. Your thumb is on one side of the bird's neck, bracing the bottom of its head, and your index finger is on the other side, doing the same. The cockatiel should look like it's resting with its back in your palm. Of course your cockatiel will be struggling, so you can place a washcloth over its feet so it can grasp onto it. A bird that tends to bite can be grasped like this using a thin towel so it can chew on it and not on your fingers.

Once you feel that you're holding your cockatiel in the proper fashion, have someone else gently extend its wing and clip the first ten feathers (the long ones at the end of the wing), beginning at the point where the primary feather coverts end—those are the feathers on the upper side of the wing that end at the midpoint of the primary flight feathers. With a sharp scissor, clip each feather, one by one, making a clean snip. Clip both wings—if you don't, your cockatiel will fly to the floor in circles and become flustered and clumsy.

Don't clip your cockatiel's wings until you've watched someone do it in person and have had them show you how to hold your bird properly and which feathers to clip. Don't take a pair of sharp scissors to your bird's wings unless you're sure of what you're doing.

Optimum Nutrition for the Well-Trained Cockatiel

Trying to train a nutritionally deficient cockatiel will make training sessions a lot harder, perhaps even impossible. An undernourished cockatiel is bound to be cranky, feel ill, and it will eventually succumb to any number of nutritionally related disorders. Cockatiels are not known to be picky eaters, but they do get used to a certain diet readily, and that means that a poor diet can be difficult to change. Feeding your cockatiel properly from the very beginning will help to keep it in top shape and keep your veterinary bills low. If you look around a pet shop it might seem that all you have to do is feed your cockatiel seeds and change its water— this diet can actually be compared to feeding a prisoner solely bread and water. Not only is an all-seed diet unhealthy, it will barely sustain a cockatiel, much less let it thrive.

We know much more about birds and their health needs than we did even 15 years ago— there's a lot of emphasis placed on good avian nutrition these days,

A healthy, varied, and nutritious diet is critical to your bird's health.

which can make the effort to feed your cockatiel properly a little confusing. There are so many different products on the market—seed mixes, pellets, supplements, treats—where should you begin? This chapter shows you a simple way to feed your cockatiel properly, and it shows you how to get the most nutrition out of the foods you offer.

STARTING YOUNG

Your baby cockatiel is used to eating a certain diet when it comes to you. It's important that you maintain this diet—any sudden change in diet can cause your baby bird to stop eating and become fussy. A cockatiel is active and has a high metabolism, and it can lose weight drastically if it doesn't eat—this is a dangerous situation. Instead of making your cockatiel go "cold turkey" on a new, better diet, begin offering new foods gradually and show your bird that they are good by nibbling on them yourself. You can't force a cockatiel to gorge on something it doesn't recognize as food, such as a leaf of kale, but if you keep offering it, day after day, the bird will eventually check out the new item. Some owners become frustrated with their birds because the bird refuses a food item for several days. It can take up to two weeks or more for a bird to begin to nibble at a new food, so if you are determined that your cockatiel try carrots, keep offering the carrots every day, even if it seems like a waste of time and carrots!

A NOTE ON CONSISTENCY

Some bird owners become very enthusiastic about their bird's diet for the first few months, making sure that it has the proper amount of everything it needs. Eventually, this enthusiasm wanes and the bird is once more on an unbalanced diet, which it quickly gets used to eating. It may be difficult, after a period of time, to get your cockatiel to eat properly again, so you want to make sure that you choose to feed a healthy diet that you can maintain. This might mean preparing foods in advance and keeping them in the freezer, or chopping veggies the night before you feed them—but all of this effort is worth it when you realize that you're doing something essential for the health of your cockatiel.

FRESH WATER

Clean, fresh water is essential to your cockatiel's well-being. You should offer bottled or filtered water only, and make sure that you refresh it at least twice a day. Leaving water in the dish too long can

Offer your cockatiel a number of different fresh veggies to see which it prefers, then try to introduce others.

cause bacteria to flourish and make your bird ill. Adding a drop or two of apple cider vinegar will help retard the growth of bacteria and is healthful for your bird as well. Supplementing the water with vitamins is not recommended—the vitamins provide bacteria with nutrients for spawning, turning your bird's water into a slimy mess.

Your cockatiel's water dish should be clean enough that you would have no problem drinking from it. You should have two sets of water dishes—one in use, and one soaking in a bleach solution and drying for use the next day. Water bottles not only tend to become clogged, they harbor bacteria in the tube and are more difficult to clean—owners also tend to change the water in them less frequently. Water tubes are also less likely to be changed as often. Instead, use a stainless steel coop cup for water—your cockatiel may bathe in it and toss its food inside, but that's what cockatiels do—you'll just have to clean it more often.

THE BASIC DIET

Most cockatiel keepers feed their cockatiels a diet based on seeds, with the addition of a bounty of fresh foods. An all-seed diet is deadly for the cockatiel, but a diet that includes seeds can be very balanced if you also offer other, more nutritious items. Seed is fatty and doesn't have all the nutrients that your cockatiel needs to remain healthy. A cockatiel eating only seed will begin to suffer from various maladies and will eventually die of them. Seed, in addition to a diet filled with healthy foods, is a fine base diet. You will find seed labeled for cockatiels at your pet store—this is the correct mix to feed your cockatiel. You can feed a "fancy" expensive mix if you notice that your cockatiel enjoys it, but most cockatiels will do fine with a plain seed mix. Remember, seeds are not *all* you are going to feed your cockatiel—I can't stress that enough.

Keep seeds in an airtight container or in the refrigerator or freezer so that they do not become contaminated with seed flies. Use a clean scoop to dole out the seed instead of dipping your bird's contaminated dish into it.

Seed Diet Versus Pelleted Diet

Some manufacturers produce a pelleted diet, which consists of small nuggets into which all of the nutrients your cockatiel needs are supposedly compacted. Pelleted diets are relatively new on the scene for parrot-type birds, having been used for poultry for many

years. The research conducted on poultry nutrition far exceeds the research done on parrot nutrition, and the life of the average pet bird far exceeds that of a frying chicken. Not much is known about the long-terms effect of birds eating these manufactured diets, but there are indications that they can cause liver and kidney damage. Furthermore, a small pellet prepared for a cockatiel is also the same pellet prepared for a parakeet, a lovebird, and a small

Green and orange fruits and vegetables are excellent staples in a bird's diet. Seeds, pasta, and even protein sources such as chicken are also important.

Seed mixes, pellets, and nuts are healthy and beneficial, but no one food source can provide for all of your bird's needs.

conure. How can it be that these very dissimilar birds can thrive on the same formula? Their metabolisms are different and their propensities toward obesity and activity are different as well.

Some avian experts recommend the use of these diets, suggesting that the bird need only to eat these nuggets and nothing else. For this active, curious cockatiel, this is a very boring proposition. Some people feeding pellets as a base diet also include produce and table foods, but this is not recommended according to the pellet manufacturers. This is not to say that you shouldn't feed pellets—they should be a nutritious, fun addition to your cockatiel's diet. Offer them in conjunction with all of the other foods you feed—variety in a bird's diet is the key to good health. Pellets are also a great addition to many bird-specific recipes, and they add a lot of nourishment to the cooked foods you offer your cockatiel. Ultimately, your avian veterinarian should be the one to determine the correct diet for your individual bird—if your bird's doctor believes that pellets are the proper base diet, then you should consider making the switch to pellets, though it is your final decision.

MAKING THE SWITCH TO PELLETS

If your veterinarian advises you to switch to a pelleted diet, you can't simply discontinue seed and expect your cockatiel to know that the pellets are food. You might inadvertently starve your cockatiel by making it go "cold turkey." Instead, begin mixing the seeds and the pellets at a 50:50 ratio for a week. The next week, mix the seeds at a 40:60 ratio, and so on, until the bowl is only filled with pellets. This may take at least a month. During this time, you should weigh your cockatiel on a gram scale to ensure that it is not losing too much weight, and you should carefully watch to make sure that it is actually eating the pellets.

VEGETABLES AND FRUITS

Vegetables are an important part of your cockatiel's diet. Veggies offer a variety of nutrients that your cockatiel needs to survive. Fruit is important as well, but it is full of sugar and can be fattening, though some fruits are so rich in nutrients, they are worth the calories. Feed produce that is dark green and orange in color—these items are rich in vitamin A, a nutrient that your cockatiel needs for good respiratory health. The following is a list of vegetables and fruits that you can offer every day. Remember, variety is key—offer as many as you can of these items daily:

asparagus	yellow pepper
beet tops	yellow squash
beets (raw or cooked)	zucchini
broccoli	
brussels sprouts	apples
carrots (raw or cooked)	apricots
celery	bananas
chard	berries
collard greens	cantaloupe
corn	cherries
dandelion	figs
endive	grapefruit
green beans	grapes
green pepper	honeydew
jalapenos	kiwi
kale	mango
mustard greens	oranges
peas	papaya
pumpkin	peaches
red pepper	pear
spinach	pineapple
watercress	plums
yams (cooked)	watermelon

Optimum Nutrition for the Well-Trained Cockatiel

Make sure to remove all fruit within a few hours of feeding it—it can spoil or attract "fruit flies," pesky little flying things that are tough to get rid of. Cooked veggies should also be removed within a few hours if you live in a warm climate.

Food and food cups should be refreshed and changed every day, in conjunction with a regular cleaning schedule.

TABLE FOODS

Your cockatiel can eat just about anything that you eat. The more healthy table foods that you can get your cockatiel to eat the better. With the exception of chocolate, avocado, rhubarb, alcohol, and salty, sugary, and fatty foods, your bird can eat everything on your plate. Share your meals, and be persistent if your bird is reluctant to try new foods— simply keep offering them and your bird's curiosity will get the best of it. It might seem like cannibalism, but your cockatiel might even enjoy a bit of turkey or chicken. Don't forget to bring a "birdy bag" home with you when you go out to eat!

SNACKS

Many of the commercially available treats are made of seeds. Cockatiels that are overfed seeds tend to become obese, especially when they do not get enough exercise. Limit seed treats to once a week—instead, treat your cockatiel to a special type of fruit or other healthy snack—this will keep your cockatiel from gorging on "candy" and keep its appetite fresh for more nutritious foods. Don't give up on treats, though—your cockatiel may enjoy the occasional sweet seed stick. Healthy, low fat snacks include air-popped popcorn, healthy cereal, whole wheat crackers (spread with peanut butter for the occasional sticky treat), and whole wheat bread. Finding out what your cockatiel loves is a great training tool. For example, if your bird loves millet spray, use it only during training sessions as a special treat for good behavior.

FAVORITE FOODS

You will find that your cockatiel chooses a couple of favorite foods. This is great if those foods are healthy and nutritious. For example, if your cockatiel's favorite foods are kale, carrots, and red peppers, you can feel free to feed them every day. If your bird's favorite foods are millet, celery, and watermelon, you might want to begin limiting those foods and offering more nutritious options—but that does not mean that you have to exclude those favorites forever.

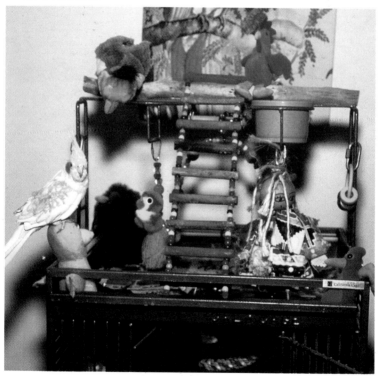

A playgym—cage-top or freestanding—can help your bird get the exercise it needs to stay fit and healthy.

A whiteface pied pearl cockatiel and its mineral block, an important supplement for many companion birds.

DIETARY SUPPLEMENTS

Some cockatiel owners add supplements to their birds' diet. Common supplements include cuttlebone, mineral block, and calcium powder. Some people drizzle supplemental oils over their birds' seeds and sprinkle supplement powder on top of that. This is not harmful for a cockatiel and can even enhance the diet. Consult your veterinarian before you begin to supplement your cockatiel's diet. A cockatiel that relishes produce, table foods, and pellets, and eats a small amount of seed should not require a supplement, though laying hens may need more calcium during breeding season.

The supplement grit that you will find in the pet shop is not recommended for cockatiels. They do not really need it and may gorge on it and become very ill and even die as a result.

EXERCISE AND NUTRITION

No discussion of nutrition would be complete without a note on exercise. You know that if you eat a completely healthy diet but do no exercise, you will not immediately become fit and trim. The same goes for your cockatiel. If your cockatiel is housed in a large cage or aviary and is allowed to fly, you can be assured that it is getting the exercise it needs—flying is the best form of exercise for a bird. If your cockatiel lives in a smallish cage or has its wings clipped, you should make sure that it gets the exercise it needs to remain healthy and fit. This means playing with your cockatiel in an active way. You can place it at the bottom of a rope or bird ladder and have it climb up, or have it climb from your hand to your shoulder as a game. Even a clipped cockatiel enjoys a good wing flapping session, and it will appreciate being out of the cage so that it can flap away without hitting a toy or the bars of its cage.

RECIPES

Cooking food for your cockatiel is a great way to provide nutritious, safe, fun foods. Here are a few recipes that you can try. You can freeze portions of each of these and thaw each day for a new, fresh treat. All of these recipes are easy and very variable—you can add whatever you happen to have in the kitchen.

Cockatiel Bread

Buy a package of corn muffin mix and follow the directions on the package. When you have the batter mixed, add a half-cup pellets, a half-cup dried fruit, a half-cup canned beans (any kind), a half-cup broccoli (or other veggie), two tablespoons of crushed cuttlebone, two

Young cockatiels, such as these cinnamon pied pearl babies, have very different nutritional requirements than their adult counterparts.

tablespoons of chunky peanut butter, and anything else you think your cockatiel might like. Bake until a knife comes out clean from the center of the bread—it may take far longer than the package recommends.

Cockatiel Pancakes

Make pancake batter the way you normally would (if you're like me, use instant), and add one cup pellets, a quarter-cup dried apricots, and a quarter-cup shredded carrots. Make like regular pancakes. You can add anything else to the batter you think your cockatiel might like.

Cockatiel Omelet

Crack several eggs into a bowl, including the shells, and add pellets, two types of chopped veggies, dried fruit, and anything else your cockatiel will like. Cook as an omelet or scramble. Cook extremely well—chicken eggs can pass on disease to parrot-type birds. Freeze into portions and then thaw enough for each day.

Cockatiel Pasta

Boil whole wheat pasta and drain. Pour it in a saucepan and melt soy cheese over it. Add pellets, veggies, bananas, crushed hard-boiled egg (including shell), or whatever else your cockatiel likes. You can freeze this in ice-cube trays and defrost a cube a day. It makes a nutritious and colorful treat!

Cockatiel Behavior

Birds are often difficult to understand—it sometimes seems that they come from another planet! This is likely due to the fact that our companion birds, including the cockatiel, are not domestic animals. A domestic animal is one that humans have changed through selective breeding to suit our needs. The cow, for example, can be bred to have a certain fat content in its flesh, or produce milk with certain desired components. Dogs are bred to accomplish certain tasks, such as herding or hunting vermin—their instincts are selected and honed by breeders. Companion birds, on the other hand, have not been changed so drastically that they have lost their natural instincts. We can understand why a Border Collie herds sheep, but we have a difficult time understanding why our cockatiels want to chew the wallpaper—this behavior seems to serve no purpose.

The cockatiel is an animal that acts out of pure instinct. It does not do things to spite you, nor does it do things to assist you—it merely acts out of a desire to fulfill its natural urges, whether that be chewing, chattering, or cuddling. The cockatiel, in general, is a lively creature that is at once loyal and territorial, and its normal behaviors can often seem bewildering to an owner who is not used to observing this special little pet. This chapter will help to take some of the confusion out of why cockatiels behave the way they do.

COCKATIEL INTELLIGENCE

The cockatiel is a bright bird, able to learn to do things all on its own, like open its cage door to escape or make a racket for attention. Do not underestimate the intelligence of this bird—it might be a bird, but it's no birdbrain! The cockatiel will learn things all on its own, but it can be stubborn about learning things you want to teach it, though most cockatiels are highly trainable. The "inability" to learn a behavior or trick does not mean that your cockatiel is a stupid bird, but that it's a highly self-directed animal, or, perhaps, that you are not teaching it correctly or with the proper amount of patience. The key to training your cockatiel is to understand your bird's limitations and to appreciate it as an individual. Luckily for the cockatiel owner, this species, although as independent as any companion bird, is easily trained with gentle, repetitive methods and patience.

VOCALIZATION

A healthy cockatiel will be highly vocal around dawn and again around dusk. In the wild, dawn is

A lone cockatiel will not thrive unless it is stimulated by toys and played with by its human companions.

the time when cockatiels are calling to one another to say, "I've made it through the night." At dusk, they call one another again to say, "Here's where I've settled to roost. I'm okay." At these times you will hear your cockatiel whistling and chirping. If you have a lone cockatiel, it is calling to you at these times and will appreciate an answer—you should call back with a whistle or just an "I'm here, everything's okay." This will help your cockatiel feel secure. If you have two or more cockatiels, you will find that they are chatting to one another—if you listen closely you will hear one bird call and the others respond.

If you are not a fan of getting up a dawn on a daily basis, you can regulate what time your cockatiel begins to vocalize by regulating the amount of light that hits the cage. You can do this by covering

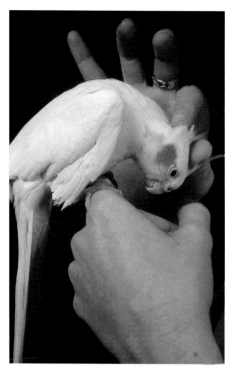

A cockatiel that offers its head and neck for scratching is one that has bonded to you and is ready to show affection.

the cage at night and uncovering it when you want in the morning, or by drawing dark curtains over your windows.

A cockatiel that is very attached to its human companion will often mimic sounds that the human makes, particularly clicking and whistling. This behavior is your cockatiel attempting to connect with you, and it indicates a bird that it very attached to its owner. Some cockatiels are able to mimic human speech well, and most are particularly good at whistling.

Cockatiels also hiss and make a spitting noise when they feel threatened. This is normal, and it is used to ward off intruders. Do not attempt to train a hissing cockatiel—you might get a nasty bite! Instead, make friends with an apprehensive cockatiel by offering millet and talking softly. Wait until the bird has calmed down before beginning a training session.

BODY LANGUAGE

You can tell a lot about how a cockatiel feels by its body language. Close observation of your cockatiel may reveal the following body language:

* Sleeping on one foot: This means that the cockatiel is healthy and content. A cockatiel sleeping on two feet may not be feeling well or may be too warm.

* Feather fluffing: A quick ruffle of the feathers signifies a content bird that is releasing tension and getting ready to perform another task, such as flying or moving to the water dish. A cockatiel that is

sitting on a perch with its feathers fluffed may be not feeling well or might be cold. If your cockatiel is fluffed, backed into a corner, wings shaking and beak open, it's displaying territorial behavior, so watch your fingers—this is a bird that's going to bite!

* The crest: When the head crest is back with the tip pointing upward and the bird is going about its business, it is at ease and comfortable. When the crest is raised, the bird may be excited, but not necessarily afraid. If the crest is standing straight up, it is a signal that the bird is anxious or distressed. If the crest is slicked down flat and the bird is crouching and hissing, the cockatiel is fearful and highly apprehensive.

* Stretching: Cockatiels stretch for the same reasons we do—because it feels good, to release tension, and to get tired muscles moving again.

* Yawning: Birds yawn to clear their nasal passages, just like we do. If you notice excessive yawning in your cockatiel, it might indicate a health problem. You may notice something that looks like a blockage in your cockatiel's nose—this is a normal part of your bird's nose, used to keep debris out of its nasal passages. Never try to remove anything from your bird's nose.

* Tail bobbing: A singing or chirping cockatiel will have a wildly bobbing tail. If your cockatiel's tail is bobbing a lot while it's resting on a perch, it could indicate a respiratory problem.

* Poop posture: A cockatiel that's about to poop will back up a little, wag its tail, and then bombs away! Get to know this posture if you want to avoid having to change your shirt!

Preening is a normal behavior that will occupy a good deal of your bird's time. However, excessive preening may be cause for concern.

NORMAL BEHAVIORS

Cockatiels can do some pretty uncanny things that will look like problem behaviors, when they are actually quite healthy and normal. Look for these normal behaviors in your cockatiel:

• Preening: Preening is when your cockatiel runs its beak through its feathers, making sure they are all clean and in place. Each feather is made up of little strands that zip together like Velcro—your cockatiel spends a lot of time making sure that each feather is zipped properly. Preening isn't just for vanity purposes. It keeps the feathers clean for flying and for insulation.

• Beak grinding: When a cockatiel is sleepy and content it will audibly grind the two parts of its beak together. Experts cannot find a distinct reason for this—cockatiels seem to do it simply because they want to.

• Beak wiping: When a cockatiel eats a particularly juicy or messy meal, it will wipe its beak along the sides of its cage or on a perch, usually the concrete conditioning perch, if one is provided. This is akin to a human wiping her face with a napkin, and it is one reason why it's a good idea to disinfect and scrub perches weekly.

• Wing flapping: Wing flapping while standing on a perch provides much needed exercise for a clipped bird. A bird that's flapping its wings might be testing out newly grown in feathers. Wing waving while chirping is a sign of a content, happy bird that's calling out to communicate with other birds or its owner.

• Door dancing: A cockatiel that is allowed frequent out-of-cage time might develop a little door-dance—it will stand in front of its cage door and move back and forth, desperately trying to get your attention. This is a sign that your cockatiel is well bonded to you.

• Flattened posture, wings shaking: This posture means that your cockatiel desperately wants something or wants to go somewhere—it is ready to take action on its desire, which may mean launching itself toward the object it wants—maybe you!

• Regurgitation: As gross as it sounds, a cockatiel that is bobbing its head in your direction may be "affectionately" regurgitating to you. This is a high compliment. Rarely will a cockatiel actually vomit on you, making a mess—it's more the thought that counts in this case.

• Head down: A cockatiel that is very bonded to you might desire a good bit of head and neck scratching, and will show you this by putting its head down for you and offering you a fluffed neck. Gently rub your bird against the feathers and circle the ear openings lightly—this may cause your cockatiel to yawn (if so, you know you're doing it right!).

• Chewing: Cockatiels are born to chew. This is a normal behavior. Don't take it as an aggressive act if your cockatiel chews your signed Picasso to bits—it's just doing what its instincts tell it to do. If you want to save your priceless antiques, provide your bird with plenty of things to chew, including store-bought toys and household items, such as toilet paper rolls (but make sure your cockatiel's head doesn't become stuck in one!).

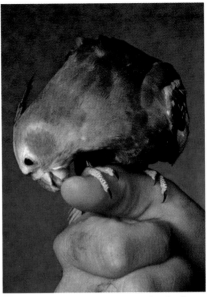

Although a cockatiel may use its beak to explore strange objects, biting or painful nips should be discouraged.

PROBLEM BEHAVIORS

Because cockatiels are not domestic animals, and their life in a home is truly a foreign experience, your pet cockatiel may acquire problem behaviors that can cause some concern in an owner who doesn't understand why the behaviors are happening or how to change them. The following are a few of the common behavior issues that cockatiels face.

• Biting: A cockatiel's beak, though not large, is very sharp and can cause bleeding to the sensitive skin on human fingers. One way to prevent biting is to play with your cockatiel every day and keep it tame. If your once-tame cockatiel is already biting, one way to *keep* it biting is to show fear and retreat every time it gnashes its beak at you. This retreat will teach the cockatiel that it is more powerful than you and that biting is a great way to get you to leave it alone. To disarm a biting cockatiel, move its cage to another room before you take it out, or gather it up in a towel and take the bird to a different location. This will distract the bird and allow you to play with it without being bitten. Once the bird sees that playing with you is fun, and that you're not afraid of it, the biting may cease, though this may take several weeks. Giving a biting cockatiel a "time out," just as

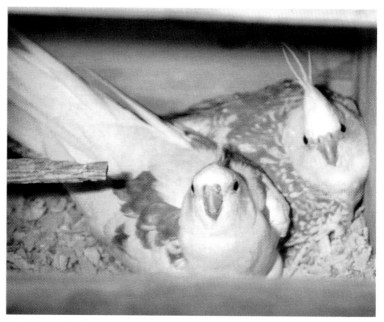

Breeding may bring on unusual behaviors such as aggression or increased territoriality, which should pass once the season ends.

you would a child having a tantrum, is a good way to teach it that biting is not going to be tolerated. Simply remove the biting bird to a small "time out" cage placed in a quiet corner—this cage shouldn't have toys or treats in it. When the bird is in this cage you will not interact with it, but wait for it to calm down and compose itself. This is often an effective method of quelling biting—the worst punishment for a bird is to ignore it. *Never* hit a bird or flick or strike the beak in any way—a bird's beak is very sensitive, and flicking it with a fingernail can really hurt and cause your bird to mistrust you. You can hold the upper part of a cockatiel's beak slightly if it persists in biting and say "no!" firmly, though most cockatiels will continue doing what they want to do anyway. A cockatiel that continues biting may not be feeling well—look for signs of illness and take your bird to the veterinarian if you suspect something is wrong.

 • Territorial display: Some cockatiels will be territorial of their cage and will defend it by charging and hissing at anyone who comes close. Often, females will lay eggs on the bottom of the cage and defend them intensely. In the case of a female laying infertile eggs, simply remove the eggs (you may need a glove to do this) and the bird should go back to her old, sweet self—until the next egg is laid. To play with a female that's displaying territorial behavior, you may have to remove her from the cage with a towel and take her to another room—the same prescription for biting applies. Realize that this territoriality is normal—it is annoying, but there's little you can do about it besides discouraging nesting behaviors.

• The jewel thief: Cockatiels adore shiny objects, and they will quickly abscond with an earring—right out of your ear! They can also break a gold chain and make off with the pendants. This is normal, though annoying behavior, and can be prevented by removing jewelry before playing with the bird.

• Self-mutilation: When a cockatiel is bored, confined, mistreated, has nutritional deficiencies, or has experienced a drastic change in its life, it may begin to pick out its feathers or chew others parts of its body, resulting in bleeding and bald patches. This is a terrible state for a cockatiel, which uses self-mutilation as a last resort to distract itself from deplorable living circumstances. Sometimes, a cockatiel that has an illness, such as a problem with its respiratory system, will pluck the feathers around the area that disturbs it. Plucking and other mutilating behaviors always need medical attention. To prevent boredom plucking, provide your cockatiel with a spacious cage and lots of different types of toys to play with and chew.

Feather picking can be caused by loneliness, boredom, mistreatment, and medical problems. Consult your avian vet for advice.

• Persistent vocalizations: A cockatiel can be

A four-month old lutino male cockatiel settles in for an enjoyable petting session from its owner.

persistently noisy, especially if it knows that its owner will come running every time it kicks up a racket. There is a difference between a cockatiel that's vocalizing normally and one that's vocalizing to get attention. Of course, you want to give your cockatiel as much attention as possible, but there will be times when you will want your bird to play independently, without expecting to be on your shoulder all day. A dark cage cover works well to quiet a noisy cockatiel, but it should not be used during the day for more than ten minutes at a time. But a cover only treats the problem, not to root of the problem. Try to find out why your cockatiel is screaming or vocalizing loudly. Perhaps something is frightening it. Perhaps you've inadvertently trained it to scream every time you leave the room by reinforcing the behavior by returning to the cage and talking to or playing with the bird. Look at your actions and see if the persistent noise is a result of something you've been doing.

• Night frights: Night fright, or night thrashing, is actually a common behavior among cockatiels, so it is not considered abnormal,

It's easier to instill good behaviors early than it is to discourage bad behaviors in adulthood.

A bird that bites may be better to tame and handle on a stick than by hand, especially with a cockatiel's sharp beak.

though you should take steps to prevent it. During night frights, a cockatiel will thrash violently around the cage, responding to noises or movement in the night. Unknown sounds or shadows can frighten the sensitive cockatiel and cause it to try to flee. To prevent thrashing, use a nightlight in your cockatiel's room and don't cover the cage completely—allow your bird to see what's going on in its surroundings. A cockatiel can injure itself during a thrashing episode; examine it carefully for broken feathers and injured feet or eyes.

• Egg laying in the single hen: Egg laying can pose a health and behavior problem in female cockatiels. A female may become depleted of calcium from laying eggs to replace the ones you remove and she can become territorial of her "nest." To prevent her from laying eggs remove anything that she might consider a nesting site and decrease the availability of light to eight or nine hours a day—this will lead her to believe that it's not breeding season. If this fails, try moving the cage to another location. Males also tend to become aggressive and will mate with their toys if they feel that it's time to breed. Use the same methods described above to keep your male's hormones in check.

CHAPTER 8

Relationship-Based Taming and Training

If you have a single cockatiel, chances are that you will want it to be tame and come out of its cage to cuddle and play with you. Once a cockatiel is bonded to an owner it is quite loyal and shows a deep affection. Training a cockatiel to be tame and playful is easy. This outgoing and sociable bird takes well to life in the average home.

Cockatiels are indeed trainable to perform certain simple behaviors, and they are even known to be good at simple "tricks." However, it is actually more likely that your cockatiel will train you

Effective training should be based on the foundation of a sound relationship. Allow your cockatiel plenty of time to get used to you.

than the other way around! You will find that your cockatiel will get you to do its bidding pretty quickly. Cockatiels are fast learners. If your cockatiel is begging to be let out of its cage with high-pitched whistles and a frantic dance in front of its door and you open the cage, it will soon learn that this method works. If you don't mind this behavior, you can continue reinforcing it by giving in to your bird; if not, ignoring the behavior is the first step to stopping it. However, you should keep these things in mind from the very beginning and work to avoid them from the start.

For optimal training, you must first develop a relationship with your cockatiel. This means that you will not force it to do anything it doesn't want to do and that you respect it as you would a good friend. A bird that views its owner as a friend is more likely to do what its owner wants it to do. In other words, fear tactics don't work with birds; gentle, patient training methods do. Make a friend of your cockatiel from the very beginning. Talk softly to it and handle it tenderly. Come to know it as an individual. Just as some humans are smarter than others or are more apt to learn certain things, so too with the cockatiel. You might have the Einstein of cockatiels, able to learn many tricks, or you may have the Forrest Gump of cockatiels, one that takes the world as it comes. Know your cockatiel's limitations before you set out to teach it complicated behaviors. Having a great relationship with your cockatiel, one that's based on mutual give and take, is better than forcing an unwilling bird to do something it's not meant to do.

HOUSEHOLD RULES

Teaching your cockatiel household rules is like teaching a two-year-old child the same—it can be done using a lot of repetition. However, some rules may never be learned, which is why cockatiels need supervision when they are out of the cage. Cockatiel-proofing your home, making it a safe place for your cockatiel to play, will help in preventing mischief and tragedy.

Create household rules for every human member of the family who interacts with the cockatiel. One member may try to train a certain behavior; another will try to teach it something different; still another may be treating the bird with impatience. Agreeing on how the cockatiel will be handled goes a long way toward proper training. Some trainers will suggest that only one person train the bird. This is ideal, but it is hardly realistic, especially if there are children involved. Everyone in the household can participate in training the bird, as long as there are ground rules to how and what the bird is learning.

Children, in particular, must be "trained" to handle the cockatiel with composure and decorum. Teach children how to treat the new bird gently and calmly from the very beginning, and supervise all young children while they are handling the bird.

TRAINING A YOUNG COCKATIEL

A very young cockatiel is easy to handle. It has not yet learned to bite, and it will be more apt to be gentle and willing to try new things. Handle your youngster every day.

Finger training will allow you to move your cockatiel around safely, as well as retrieve it in the event that it gets loose in the house.

Cuddle and play with it. When it begins to nip at your hands or your neck, even if the bird is just playing, you must stop it from nibbling and tell it "no!" in a firm voice. Little nibbles from a youngster will turn into hard biting when the bird gets a little older. Preventing bad behavior in a youngster will avoid you having to train the behavior out of it once the bird gets older. It is far easier to train a good behavior *into* a bird than it is to stop a bird from doing something it has grown used to. Using the "no!" command is generally effective in stopping a behavior at the moment, but the bird often goes right back to doing what it wants to do. Keeping a close eye on your cockatiel will help to prevent mischief and trouble.

TAMING THE SEMI-TAME COCKATIEL

A semi-tame cockatiel is one that has experience with humans but is not all that trustful of them. This bird can be tamed easily if you take steps to develop a trusting relationship with it. There are two ways to tame a cockatiel: you can "break" it or you can "gentle" it.

Using a gentle, slow training method is always preferable with animals, especially those as sensitive as cockatiels. Breaking a cockatiel using quick, violent training might work for a time, but it won't allow a real bond to form between you and your cockatiel. Your cockatiel will always be wary of you, and cockatiels have excellent memories.

When you first bring your semi-tame cockatiel home you will want to give it a period of adjustment. Your bird will be stressed in its new situation and may even flap around the cage when you approach. Do not consider taming it until it has settled into a routine. This may take a few days to a couple of weeks. Once a cockatiel is eating well, vocalizing, preening, and bathing, it is adjusted to its new home.

Treats may be the most effective reward for training, but don't overlook the use of enthusiastic praise.

Once the cockatiel has settled in, you can begin taming. You will first need to clip the bird's wings. A cockatiel with free flight will simply fly away from you and not return. Even if you eventually want to allow your bird to fly, you will have to clip the wings during the training period—the feathers will grow back in time if you want them to.

Once the bird's wings are clipped you can begin the taming process. With a small towel, remove your bird from its cage and hold it gently in the towel to prevent it from biting you. It may scream and struggle, but you should continue to be calm and talk to it in a low, soothing voice. Take the bird to a small room—a bathroom is ideal, but be sure to close the toilet lid and remove any dangerous items that may fall and break if the bird comes in contact with them. Sit on

Relationship-Based Taming and Training

the floor with your knees bent into "mountains" and place the bird gently on top of one of your knees, holding it there for a moment before you let go. The moment you let go the bird will probably flutter away from you in a desperate escape attempt. Gather up the bird again and try to place it on your knee again. Repeat this action until the bird eventually stands there for a moment. Remember to remain calm. The bird may not want to stand on your knee in the first few sessions, but keep trying. You can do this twice a day for 20 minutes each session, but no more than that. You want to begin to build trust with the bird, not stress it out.

Once you've reached the point when your bird will stand on your knee, talk to it in a very calm voice and begin to move one hand slowly up your leg toward the bird. This may cause it to flutter off of your knee again. No matter—simply try again. Little by little, session after session, move your hand slowly up your leg until the bird allows it to come very close. The idea here is that the bird should eventually allow contact with your hand. This may take quite a while, so be patient. Once the bird allows your hand to approach closely, try to tickle its chest with your finger or scratch its head and neck if it allows, still moving very slowly. After a few sessions of doing this you

The step-up command is the most important behavior you can teach your cockatiel; be certain you are both comfortable with its use.

can begin to try to get the bird to stand on your hand. Remember, all of this should be done with a lot of patience. Using low lighting in the bathroom can often help.

At the end of the training session, place your cockatiel back in its cage—if you have trouble doing this, put your hand gently over the bird's back—this way it can't open its wings to try to fly away or attempt to climb on the cage. Give it a treat and tell it how good a bird it was. After a few moments you can allow it out for independent playtime.

DISCIPLINE

Proper discipline for a bird consists of one method—ignoring it. This is the worst punishment for a bird. It will learn very quickly that it doesn't get to play if it bites or screams. Placing a biting bird in a time-out cage for a few minutes is a good way to show it that you're not thrilled with its behavior. After a particularly unwanted behavior, you can ignore your bird for up to ten minutes—this will give it the right idea. Don't ignore the bird for long periods of time because that can be very stressful for this flock-oriented animal.

There are a few things you should never do to your cockatiel during training, or at any other time. Any improper discipline will only

Although some owners use a harness to restrain their birds outdoors, such devices are not foolproof, and they do not ensure your pet's full safety.

With two owners in a household it's a good idea to use similar training techniques, to keep from confusing a bird.

result in breaking the trust that you and your cockatiel need to build in order to have a mutually satisfying relationship.

* Never hit, flick, squeeze, or throw your cockatiel. This is animal abuse and will make your cockatiel mistrust you.

* Never throw anything at your cockatiel's cage to make it stop vocalizing. Throwing things at the cage will make your cockatiel feel very insecure.

* Never "play rough" with your cockatiel. This will teach it to be aggressive and to bite.

* Never cover the cage for long periods during the day. If you have a sleeping infant or you simply need your bird to quiet down, you can cover the cage for an hour or so, but it's cruel to cover it for extended periods when your cockatiel should be active.

* Never starve your cockatiel as a training tool. Sure, your bird will be hungry and might do what you want it to do for a sunflower seed, but this might backfire on you and cause your bird to become ill. Cockatiels have high metabolisms and can have seizures and even die if their blood sugar drops too low.

* Never be afraid of your cockatiel. Even if you are afraid, don't show it that you are. Pulling your hand away from a bird that's bluffing a bite will teach it that it's powerful and that it can threaten you.

Instead, use a stick or dowel to take the bird out of the cage—you should stick train your bird as soon as possible.

TEACHING THE STEP-UP COMMAND

Of all the behaviors you can teach your cockatiel, the step-up command is possibly the most important. This command allows you to retrieve your cockatiel at any time, and it is especially useful when your bird is fussy or is in potential danger. *Step-up* is the act of your cockatiel stepping gently on to your hand or finger, without hesitation, on command. A cockatiel is not hatched knowing how to do this, so you must teach it. Perhaps your cockatiel came to you already tame and hand trained—that's great! But it's still important to reinforce the step-up command so that it becomes second nature to you and to your cockatiel.

Assuming that you are teaching a tame or semi-tame cockatiel the step-up command, begin by allowing the cockatiel to come out of its cage on its own. You win nothing by fishing the cockatiel out violently, and you will only succeed in beginning your training session on a bad note. Place a perch on top of its cage, or let the bird climb on to a standing perch where it will be standing on a round dowel, not a flat surface. If your cockatiel is a youngster, you can gently lift it out of the cage, but because it doesn't yet know how to step up, be careful not to pull too hard on its feet—it will grip the perch, not understanding what you want.

Once the cockatiel is out, give it a treat, either a bit of yummy food or a good head scratching. This will show the bird that training sessions can be fun, and it will look forward to them. Next, begin rubbing your bird's chest and belly very softly and gently with the length of your index finger, cooing to it, slowly increasing the pressure with which you push on its chest. You may have to repeat this for a few days, depending on the tameness of your cockatiel. Your semi-tame cockatiel may not be sure what you are up to, and it might be wary of this attention. Take things slowly and work to gain its trust. A tamer cockatiel will often sit quietly, enjoying the attention.

Once you feel that your cockatiel is calm and used to this process, you can increase the pressure you place on its chest. Pushing slightly on a cockatiel's chest will throw it off balance, and it will lift up a foot to right itself. Place your finger or hand under the foot and lift the bird, if it allows it. If not, simply allow its foot to remain on your hand until the bird removes it. As you do this, tell your bird clearly to "step-up." You must always say "step-up" when it steps on to your hand—it is key that your cockatiel associates the action of stepping onto your hand with the phrase.

Once your cockatiel is fairly good at stepping up, you can have it step it from finger to finger, repeating the phrase "step-up" and praising it. Your bird may hesitate at first, but soon it will know exactly what you want. Be sure that your training sessions last only a few minutes each, and try not to become frustrated if your cockatiel doesn't do exactly what you want right away. Training sessions are ideally short, perhaps 10 to 15 minutes twice a day, and they should be incorporated into playtime.

Most youngsters will learn the step-up command easily, in one or two short sessions, while a semi-tame cockatiel will take longer—the more your cockatiel trusts you, the easier it will be to teach it anything. Remember, patience is key. Even if this command is the only "trick" you teach your cockatiel, it is by far the most valuable. If you make sure to say "step-up" every time you lift your cockatiel, you will reinforce this important training every day and it will make life much easier for both of you.

STICK TRAINING

Stick training is simply teaching the "step-up" command using a perch or dowel instead of your finger. It is very important that your cockatiel know how to step onto a stick. The day may come when your cockatiel refuses to come down from the curtain rod, or gets out of the house and is sitting high in a tree, chirping away. A cockatiel that has been stick trained will be easy to retrieve with a long dowel or broomstick. A cockatiel that is not used to stepping on a stick will be

Although cockatiels are not known as the most proficient talkers, with some enthusiasm and practice yours may learn a word or two.

terrified of it and you may lose the opportunity to save your bird from harm. Teach "step-up" with a stick the same way you teach it with your finger. Stick training should begin as soon as you begin hand taming your cockatiel. If your bird is terrified of the stick, you can leave it close to the cage where your bird will have a chance to view it and get used to its presence. Use different sticks during training so that your cockatiel learns not to be afraid of various dowels and perches.

TAMING THE BRONCO COCKATIEL

The bronco cockatiel is one that has not had much, if any, handling by humans. It is generally fearful of humans and can be aggressive, but it is not impossible to tame. The first thing you have to do with the bronco, after letting it adjust to its new home, is show it that you are not afraid of it. The bronco bird will want nothing more than to be left alone, and it will show you this by hissing and biting. If you are bitten and you retreat, you show the bird that it has the upper hand. The best way to deal with biting is to avoid being bitten. This means that you may want to work with stick training before you begin using your hands. Putting on thick gloves will only frighten your cockatiel more and hinder training, so try to avoid them.

Being afraid of your cockatiel's beak is an understandable fear, especially when the bird is untamed. If this is the case, try the "whittle down" method. Begin by stick training your bird with the step-up command using a 12- to 18-inch dowel or perch—use a width sized appropriately for a cockatiel. Once your bird learns to step on to the stick and does it with ease, begin cutting the stick down, about an inch each week, until the stick is very short. Eventually, if you've done this slowly enough and have worked to gain your bird's trust, the stick will be so short that your cockatiel will step onto your hand.

If your cockatiel is really wild, you can use the towel method for the first few training sessions. Hold the bird properly and gently in a towel and talk softly to it while caressing its head. Do this twice a day for the first few days before you begin training in the bathroom. This will show your cockatiel that you are not to be feared and that you mean no harm. Use this method *only* if you are certain that holding your cockatiel is not causing it pain or undue stress, and do it only for a few minutes at a time.

TEACHING YOUR COCKATIEL TO TALK

Many male cockatiels will learn to talk simply by listening to the words that you say most often, such as the bird's name, hello, and so on. The words that you repeat most often will be the words that your bird picks up, especially if they contain the letters b, p, t, c, and k. These hard-sounding letters seem to be easy for birds to learn. If you want your bird to learn to say a specific word or phrase, simply repeat it clearly, over and over, preferably in a high-pitched voice. You can make a tape of yourself saying the phrase and leave it on when you are gone. You can also buy tapes and CDs that are specifically made to help birds learn to speak, although these are not as effective as teaching birds to speak yourself.

Female cockatiels might pick up a word or two, but it is more likely that they will learn to whistle. Both males and females are proficient whistlers. You can buy a tape or CD of whistles to teach either sex to whistle.

If you want a cockatiel that is potentially a good talker, watch a group of cockatiels at the pet store. If one is particularly noisy or vocal, there is a chance that this bird may make a better talker than the others.

TRICK TRAINING

Cockatiels can be taught simple tricks, but they are not known to be highly proficient at learning complicated behaviors, the way a larger bird might. You might become frustrated trying to teach your

Consider potty training as an option, especially if you intend to allow your cockatiel a lot of free time on your furniture and possessions.

TAMING AND TRAINING COCKATIELS **81**

cockatiel to ride a bicycle, but you might be satisfied with teaching it to place an object in a cup, climb a rope, or ring a bell.

The best way to teach your cockatiel tricks is to capitalize on its natural behaviors. For example, if you notice that your cockatiel is wonderful at climbing, place it on the end of a long piece of rope and encourage it to climb up, praising it in a high-pitched voice when it completes the task. Remember, whenever you want to teach your cockatiel anything, use a lot of praise and make the training session fun. Also, if you can find a treat that your cockatiel adores, millet spray, for example, use it in your training sessions rather than just offering it freely in the cage.

POTTY TRAINING

Birds don't have the ability to "hold it" the way humans do. A bird must be light in order to fly, so nature designed them such that any added weight is eliminated quickly. Potty training isn't difficult, but you must realize that there will be accidents, and that they are okay. Praise your bird for a job well done, and ignore (and clean up!) the unwanted "behavior."

Begin potty training by recognizing the signs just before your bird poops. Usually, a bird will back up or squat a bit, lift the tail, and let the poop fly. Each time your bird poops, say "go poop" or some other tasteful phrase. Your bird will come to associate the act of pooping with the command. After a few days of this, stop your bird "mid-poop" by picking the bird up the moment your recognize these signs. Then place it in the desired "pooping place" and tell it to "go poop." If your bird does well, praise it lavishly. Another option is to place something under your bird—a paper plate or a sheet of newspaper—and asking it to "go poop" on to the item. The bird will eventually learn that it must poop where or when you want it to.

There is a danger, however, in enforcing this command too strictly. For example, if a cockatiel is trained to only poop in its cage and you board it or change its cage, it may not know to poop there and will hold the poop in, which may cause it to become ill, or at the very least, quite stressed.

CHAPTER 9

Beyond Good Health

You will only have a well-trained cockatiel if you have a healthy and happy cockatiel. There's no bird less trainable than an ill bird, and such a bird will do everything in its power to get you to leave it alone. Here are a few good tips to help you keep your cockatiel in prime condition.

GROOMING

Grooming your bird is one step you can take to keep it healthy and safe. Grooming a bird consists of clipping the flight feathers, keeping the toenails trimmed, and making sure that the beak is properly aligned and isn't growing too long. If you play with your cockatiel regularly you might notice that its toenails pinch and prick you uncomfortably. This is the time to trim its toenails. If your cockatiel has a conditioning perch made of concrete or another rough material, you may only have to trim the toenails three or four times a year. Your cockatiel's toenails

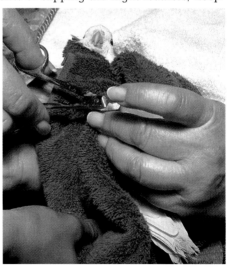

For those willing to learn, nail trimming is one of the grooming chores that you can undertake yourself.

should have a graceful half-moon curve to them—if they extend beyond this, your bird might have a medical problem related to a nutritional deficiency or could potentially have mites. See your veterinarian if your cockatiel's toenails seem unusual in any way.

A bird's toenails are like our toenails—there's a dead part and a living part, called the quick. When trimming your bird's nails you only want to cut off the dead part of the nail. Cutting into the quick is very painful and causes bleeding. Because of this, you will want to trim the nails very conservatively. In a bird with clear or pink nails, it will be easy to see the quick (the darker, blood-filled part) and avoid cutting into it. In a bird with dark nails you will only want to take off the very tip of the nail. You can use a small human nail clipper to trim the nails, which may be a two-person job—one to hold the bird properly and one to trim the nails. If bleeding does occur, simply apply styptic power to the wound and it should stop.

There should never be a reason for you to groom your cockatiel's beak. Eating hard items, chewing toys, and grooming its beak on a conditioning perch will all help to keep the beak trimmed and properly aligned. In some cases, when a cockatiel is ill or has a severe nutritional deficiency or mites, the beak may become elongated and may interfere with eating. This is a case for a veterinarian's treatment. You can severely injure your cockatiel by trying to trim the beak yourself.

MOLTING

When birds molt they shed their feathers and make way for new ones to grow. The old feathers may have become ragged and not useful for insulation or flying anymore. A molt can happen once or twice a year, depending on the amount of light and warmth your cockatiel is exposed to, and it is a very stressful time for a bird. Your cockatiel may become ill-tempered and not want to be touched at certain times. The newly growing feathers can be uncomfortable or tender. You will notice little "pins" beginning to poke out from between your cockatiel's other feathers. These are called pin feathers. The "pin" is a sheath of material (keratin) that protects the new feather until it is ready to emerge. Your cockatiel will spend time removing these sheathes, but will not be able to remove the ones on its head—if your bird allows head scratching, you can gently remove them just as a mate would.

Molting birds do not lose all of their feathers at once. Most molts are many weeks or months long, and feathers are replaced gradually. If

A gentle spray bath encourages natural grooming and is a treat for most birds, especially those that are molting.

you notice bald patches on your cockatiel's body or its feathers become so thin you can see the skin beneath them, take your bird to your avian veterinarian right away—there may be a serious problem.

Pin feathers and new feathers that have just emerged from the sheath have a blood supply and will bleed if injured or broken, which can happen easily with cockatiels that experience night thrashing. Breakage often happens with a wing feather, especially in a clipped bird, which does not have fully grown wing feathers that would protect a new feather from breaking. If you notice a bleeding feather, perhaps one that was clipped during wing trimming, don't panic. Pull the feather straight out from the root with one quick motion and the bleeding will stop immediately. A pair of needle-nosed pliers is good for this purpose and should be kept in your bird first aid kit. If you're squeamish about this, apply styptic powder to the bleeding area and take your bird to your avian veterinarian as soon as possible.

Regular misting with warm water is helpful in softening the pin feathers. Only mist your bird in temperate weather and when there's adequate time for it to dry before evening. Offer your cockatiel an extra-nutritious diet while it's molting, including a protein source, such as hard-boiled eggs, egg food, and boiled chicken. You shouldn't notice any difference in the way your cockatiel behaves, eats, plays, or responds to you during a molt, but there is the possibility for it to behave differently while the new feathers are emerging.

BATHING YOUR COCKATIEL

If you offer your cockatiel water in a coop cup it will bathe itself, splashing water all over the cage and surrounding area. Some very tame cockatiels will enjoy bathing in a soft stream of water coming from the kitchen sink's tap and some will even enjoy sitting on a special perch while their owner is showering. A mister simulating rain is a good way to get your cockatiel to bathe as well. Bathing is important for your cockatiel not only because it keeps the bird clean, but because it encourages preening. You bird only needs clean, fresh water for bathing. There are bathing products that you can buy from the pet shop, but they are not really necessary. Bathe your bird only in warm weather and in the daytime, allowing plenty of time for it to dry thoroughly. Never use soaps or other detergents.

KEEPING YOUR COCKATIEL HEALTHY

Once you acquire your new cockatiel, you should make an appointment in the first three days to see an avian veterinarian near you. An avian veterinarian is a doctor who has been trained to treat the illnesses and injuries of birds. The avian veterinarian has experience with recognizing and treating illnesses particular to birds, whose bodily systems are far different from those of a dog or cat. Your avian veterinarian is your first line of defense in keeping your cockatiel healthy. A "well-bird" checkup will ensure that your bird is healthy, and it will begin a relationship with the doctor that will last the lifetime of your bird. Many veterinarians will not treat emergencies unless the patient is already registered at the office, so you might find yourself in a dire situation if you haven't created this valuable relationship.

Take your cockatiel to the avian veterinarian at least once a year, around the same time. This will enable the doctor to weigh the bird and to perform routine tests, which will show any changes and indicate any potential disorders. This is also a good time to discuss your bird's diet and have the doctor trim its nails.

Choosing an avian veterinarian takes a bit more effort than just finding one near your home. Make sure that the doctor has a good bedside manner and is open to your questions and concerns. Ask the veterinarian if she has birds of her own. Find out what hours the office is open, and what the emergency policy is. Find an avian veterinarian that will speak to you in the middle of the night should your bird become injured. When you visit the office, look around to make sure that it's clean and talk to the staff to see if they are friendly and efficient.

You can locate an avian veterinarian by calling the Association of Avian Veterinarians at 561-393-9801 or by going to their website at www.aav.com. The American Federation of Aviculture at 602-484-0931 or on the internet at www.afa.birds.org also has information on how to find an avian veterinarian in your area.

It's best to find an avian vet before or soon after you bring your cockatiel home—and certainly before any emergencies arise.

SIGNS AND SYMPTOMS OF AN ILL COCKATIEL

Cockatiels, like most birds, tend to hide their illnesses until a disease is quite advanced. A wild cockatiel that shows itself to be ill is vulnerable to predators and will try to behave as normally as possible for as long as possible—your cockatiel has the same idea. Knowing what to look for in an ailing cockatiel will help you to recognize the illness early, which is key to treatment and speedy recovery.

* Excessive sleeping: An ill cockatiel may sleep too much, especially during the day. Sleeping on the bottom of the cage is particularly significant.

* Fluffed-up appearance: If you notice that your cockatiel is fluffy, it may be trying to maintain its body temperature and could be fighting off an illness.

* Loss of appetite: You should know how much food and what

types of food your cockatiel is consuming each day. If you notice that your bird is not eating or is eating far less than usual, it could be ill.

* Change in attitude: If your cockatiel seems listless and is not behaving in its usual manner, for example, if it has become cranky or limp, call your veterinarian.

* Lameness: If your cockatiel can't use its feet or hold up its head there's something wrong. Possible reasons include injury and egg binding. Consult an avian veterinarian immediately.

* Panting or labored breathing: These symptoms might signify a respiratory illness or overheating.

* Discharge: If you notice runniness or discharge on the eyes, nares, or vent, there may be an illness present.

* Change in droppings: Your cockatiel's droppings should consist of a solid green portion, white urates (overlapping the green portion), and a clear liquid. If the droppings are discolored (very dark green, black, yellow, or red) and there has been no change in diet (such as feeding beets or blueberries), there might be a problem. Also, if there's a pungent odor or the droppings seem far more liquid than usual, call your veterinarian immediately.

* Debris around the face or on feathers: Indicates poor grooming or regurgitation, both of which are potential signs of illness.

* Seizures: If your cockatiel is flailing in its cage and there are no obvious signs of it being caught in parts of its cage or a toy, and it's not a night fright, rush to your avian vet.

* Severe change in feather quality or quantity: If your cockatiel begins to lose feathers in patches or you notice it picking them out, call your veterinarian for an appointment. Note that many lutino cockatiels have

Getting your cockatiel used to being handled in a towel will make it easier to handle the bird for grooming or if it becomes injured.

a bald spot under the crest— this is completely normal.

QUARANTINE

Quarantine is traditionally a period of 40 days in which a new bird is kept separate from birds already established in the household—some people choose to shorten this period to 30 days and find no harm in doing so. During the period of quarantine a new bird is watched for signs of illness. You should feed and water the new bird after you care for your other birds, and change your clothing and disinfect your hands after any contact with the bird or its cage. Quarantine is the only way to prevent a new bird from passing a potential illness to the birds you already own. It is sometimes not possible to com-

Excessive sleeping is an indication of illness; contact a vet if your bird seems lethargic, especially if it is sleeping on the floor of its cage.

pletely separate a new bird from established birds, but you should try to do your best to keep contact at a minimum while the new bird is being quarantined.

TIPS FOR COMMON EMERGENCIES

Sometimes it's not easy to get to an avian veterinarian right away after an emergency has occurred, so you will have to comfort and treat your cockatiel on your own until you can get to the doctor's office. The following is a list of tips for dealing with common emergencies.

Creating a Hospital Cage

A hospital cage is important to have on hand for many emergencies and illnesses. It's a comfortable, warm, safe place for your cockatiel to calm down and recuperate from a trauma or sickness. Simply line a ten-gallon aquarium with paper towels and place a heating

Any injury to the eye should be considered serious enough to warrant an emergency call to an avian veterinarian.

pad on low to medium underneath one half of the aquarium—your bird must be able to move away from the heat if it gets too warm. Cover the aquarium with a mesh aquarium cover and drape a towel over three-quarters of the tank. Place a *very* shallow dish of water (a weak bird can drown in even an inch of water) in the cage, as well as some millet spray and seeds or pellets. Do not include toys or perches, but you can include a rolled up hand towel for snuggling. Place the cage in a quiet location and clean the papers once a day or when they become soiled.

Contact With Poison

If your bird comes in contact with poison and you notice evidence of vomiting, paralysis, seizures, shock, or bleeding from the eyes, nares, mouth, or vent, and you're not able to get to an avian veterinarian right away, call the National Animal Poison Control Center 24-hour Poison Hotline at 800-548-2423, 888-4-ANIHELP or 900-680-0000 and ask for their help. You will need to have an idea of the poison your bird has ingested. Note that there is a fee for this service.

Broken Blood Feathers

Sometimes a wing or tail feather will break in the middle of the growth process and begin to bleed. This is not a serious injury and you can deal with it yourself. Keep a styptic powder or pencil on hand and apply the product until the bleeding has stopped. Next, you will need to remove the feather from the skin with a pair of needle-nosed pliers.

Beyond Good Health

While restraining the bird (you may need two people for this procedure), simply grasp the broken feather with the pliers, close to the shaft, and pull straight out. This will stop the bleeding and prevent infection. If you are too squeamish to do this yourself, take your cockatiel to your avian veterinarian.

Oil on the Feathers

If your cockatiel becomes soaked in oil it will no longer be able to regulate its body temperature, a condition that can be deadly. Dust the oil-soaked bird with cornstarch or flour, then gently bathe it in a small tub of warm water and some mild grease-fighting dish soap. Don't scrub the bird. You may have to repeat this process several times. Keep the bird in a warm hospital cage until most of the oil is removed and the bird is dry.

Immediate Response to Overheating

An overheated cockatiel will pant and spread its wings, trying to cool itself. If this is unsuccessful and the heat does not abate, the bird may lose consciousness and even die. If you notice that your cockatiel is becoming overheated, remove it immediately to a cooler place and run a fan near its cage. Lightly mist the bird with cool water and offer drops of cool water in its mouth. Never set a cock-

Breeding females need special nutrient-rich foods and extra calcium to maintain strength and health.

atiel out in the sun unless it has a shady spot to retreat to, and never leave a cockatiel in a closed car on a warm day—birds are easily overcome by heat, far quicker than a dog.

Response to Egg Binding

Occasionally a female cockatiel will become calcium deficient or have a disorder of the reproductive tract and an egg will become stuck inside her. This can cause paralysis and even death if left untreated. If you notice your female bird fluffed on the bottom of her cage, panting, and she has a distended belly and her droppings are large and watery, she may be trying to lay an egg. Give her some time to lay it on her own, but if 24 hours pass and she hasn't laid it, you may need to intervene. If you can't get her to an avian veterinarian right away, place a few drops of mineral oil or olive oil in her vent (just at the outside of it) and a couple of drops in her mouth. This may help to lube the area and ease the egg out. If that doesn't work, try it again and move her into a very warm hospital cage and call your avian veterinarian. Even if she passes the egg, she might need an examination so that the situation doesn't occur again.

YOUR COCKATIEL'S FIRST AID KIT

Here is a list of essential items for a bird first aid kit. Keep these items in a small tackle box for convenient access when you need them.

Antibiotic ointment (for small wounds, use a non-greasy product only—oil prevents a bird from keeping in body heat)

Eyewash

Bandages and gauze

Bottled water (you may need clean, fresh water to flush out a wound or clean your bird of debris)

Baby bird formula (can be used for adults having a difficult time eating)

Cotton balls

Cotton swabs

Non-greasy first aid lotion

Dishwashing detergent (mild, for cleaning oil off of feathers)

Heating pad (always allow your bird the option of moving off of the heating pad)

Hydrogen peroxide (always use in a weak solution with water)

Nail clippers

Styptic powder, used to stop a nail or broken feather from bleeding, is a must for any companion bird's first aid kit.

Nail file
Needle-nosed pliers (for broken blood feathers)
Penlight
Electrolyte solution, for human babies (for reviving a weak bird)
Saline solution
Sanitary wipes
Sharp scissors
Syringe (without needle)
Styptic powder (to stop bleeding)
Small, clean towels (for holding or swabbing)
Spray bottle (for misting)
Alcohol (for sterilizing tools)
Tweezers
Small transport cage
Veterinarian's phone number
A sealed bag or can of your bird's base diet (in case of evacuation)

Resources

AFA Watchbird
American Federation of Aviculture,Inc.
P.O. Box 56218
Phoenix, AZ 85079
www.afa.birds.org
A nonprofit organization dedicated to the promotion of aviculture and the conservation of avian wildlife through captive breeding programs, scientific research, and education (publishes a bi-monthly magazine called AFA Watchbird).

American Cockatiel Society Inc.
P.O. Box 609
Fruitland Park, FL 34731
www.acstiels.com
An organization dedicated to education—for the pet owner, breeder, and exhibitor—since 1976.

Association of Avian Veterinarians
P.O. Box 811720
Boca Raton, FL 33481
561-393-8901
www.aav.org
AAV membership is comprised of veterinarians from private practice, zoos, universities and industry, veterinary educators, researchers and technicians, and veterinary students. Serves as resource for bird owners who are looking for certified avian veterinarians.

Bird Talk
Subscription Dept.
P.O. Box 57347
Boulder, CO 80323
www.animalnetwork.com
A monthly magazine noted for its directory of avian breeders, as well as its informative articles and columns on health care, conservation, and behavior.

Bird Times
Pet Publishing, Inc.
7-L Dundas Circle
Greensboro, NC 27407
www.birdtimes.com
A source of entertaining and authoritative information about birds; articles include bird breed profiles, medical reports, training advice, bird puzzles and stories about special birds.

The Gabriel Foundation
P.O. Box 11477
Aspen, CO 81612
www.thegabrielfoundation.org
A nonprofit organization promoting education, rescue, adoption, and sanctuary for parrots.

Midwest Avian Research Expo (MARE)
10430 Dewhurst Rd.
Elyria, OH 44036
www.mare-expo.org
A nonprofit group dedicated to education and fundraising for avian research projects.

National Cockatiel Society
286 Broad St., Suite 140
Manchester, CT 06040
www.cockatiels.org
A nonprofit group dedicated to providing information on the proper care, handling, maintenance, and breeding of cockatiels.

Index

Photo credits:

Joan Balzarini 11, 59
Susan Chamberlain 85
Isabelle Francais 15, 30, 31, 35, 37, 44, 48, 49, 55, 83
M. Gilroy 19, 61
Eric Ilasenko 12, 34, 51, 67, 75, 76
Bonnie Jay 10, 27, 29, 32, 38, 39, 42, 43, 52, 62, 63, 69, 71, 77, 79, 87, 88, 93
Robert Pearcy 14, 16
Rafi Reyes 4, 13
John Tyson 6, 7, 8, 17, 21, 22, 23, 24, 25, 41, 47, 53, 57, 65, 66, 68, 70, 73, 74, 81,
    89, 90, 91